THE REFERRAL MAGNET

GROWING YOUR FINANCIAL PRACTICE
THROUGH THE PEOPLE YOU ALREADY KNOW

THE
REFERRAL
MAGNET

KELLY EDWARDS

LIONCREST
PUBLISHING

THE REFERRAL MAGNET

Growing Your Financial Practice Through the People You Already Know

ISBN   978-1-5445-0973-0 *Hardcover*

978-1-5445-0972-3 *Paperback*

978-1-5445-0971-6 *Ebook*

978-1-5445-0974-7 *Audiobook*

This book is dedicated to Coby, Dane, and Aspen. There is nothing more important to me in this world than our family, and it is because of your belief in me that this book exists. Thank you for helping me make it happen. I love you forever, for always, no matter what.

CONTENTS

INTRODUCTION 9

PART I: BUILDING A REFERABLE BRAND
1. REFERRALS WILL MAKE OR BREAK YOUR BUSINESS............... 21
2. BEING REFERABLE 37
3. KNOW YOUR TARGET MARKET 57
4. BUILDING YOUR BRAND.. 75
5. HIRE ROCK STAR TALENT 95

PART II: PASSING THE TEST YOU DON'T KNOW YOU'RE TAKING
6. RELATIONSHIP MARKETING 101................................. 117
7. BRAND MESSAGING 131
8. WEBSITES 159
9. SOCIAL MEDIA 179
10. EMAIL MARKETING AND NEWSLETTERS.................... 217
11. BOOSTING YOUR CREDIBILITY 231
12. ROLL OUT THE RED CARPET.................................... 249

CONCLUSION... 265
ACKNOWLEDGMENTS 269
ABOUT THE AUTHOR 271

INTRODUCTION

"How do you get new clients?" That's one of the first questions I ask every financial advisor who hires me, and the vast majority give me some variation of the same answer.

"I know this is bad, but they're mostly just referrals. I know I should be doing marketing; I just never have. But that's why I've hired you!"

I love hearing that answer, and not because it means I'm getting a new client. I love it because it means I'm about to give them a big paradigm shift, and it's going to be the first step in a process I love—turning them into a Referral Magnet.

Most advisors think of their referrals as a naturally occurring thing, and if they *really* want to grow their business, they need to do marketing to reach people they have no connection to. In most industries, they'd be right, but this is not like most industries.

THE ANOMALY OF ADVISOR MARKETING

Over the last twenty years, I've done marketing for lots of different industries. From real estate to restaurants, from hotels to hospitals, I've done it all, and I can tell you that advisor marketing is truly unique for several reasons.

First of all, in most other industries, the sky is the limit when it comes to how you're allowed to market your business, but it's not that simple in the financial world. There are rules—lots and lots of rules—from FINRA, the SEC, brokers, and more. Trust me, I work with compliance on behalf of my clients every day, so I know how frustrating all the rules can be and how hard it is to keep up as they change. You can't just listen to a marketing podcast or read a hot new marketing book and implement what you learn; you have to figure out what you're allowed to do and how you're allowed to do it.

The restrictions really complicate things, and marketing is complicated enough in the digital era. Twenty years ago, when I started my career, digital marketing was just a small segment of the industry. Now it *is* the industry. It's the dominant form of marketing today, and the platforms and methods are constantly changing. There's always something new around the corner, and it's hard for advisors to keep up with what they should be doing and whether they're allowed to do it.

The rules and restrictions definitely complicate things, but that's not the main reason advisor marketing is an anomaly. It's because of what's at stake when someone is looking for an advisor.

Think about this for a second. If you were deciding where to go for lunch today, how would you make the decision? How much time and energy would you put into choosing the restaurant? If you're like most people, it would just come down to what's convenient and sounds good. What if you were deciding where to take your spouse for a special anniversary dinner? Would it still be a spur-of-the-moment decision based on what was most convenient and sounded good? Hopefully not! If you value your marriage, you'd probably plan ahead, ask for recommendations, and maybe read some reviews. Your approach would be different because there's more at stake.

Now think about how you'd approach an even bigger decision, like what city to move to. You'd research the schools, the crime rates, the cost of living, and the distance from work. You'd probably talk to people who live there to see how they like it, and drive around to see the shops, restaurants, and parks. You'd go through a very different decision-making process than you would for choosing a restaurant because the stakes are much higher.

When someone is looking for a financial advisor, they're looking for someone to help them grow and protect everything they've worked so hard for. What's at stake is their lifestyle, their legacy, and their ability to provide for themselves and the people they love. A good or bad decision could impact their financial security for the rest of their lives, and that's why it's not a decision people take lightly.

They're not just going to pick an advisor because their office is nearby or because they saw an ad on Facebook. They're going to do their due diligence to make sure they choose an advisor who knows what they're doing and is trustworthy to look after their best interests. That's why marketing for financial advisors is so different from any other industry. Instead of starting the process with a Google search for "financial advisor near me," most people start the process by asking people they know and trust, "Who is your advisor?"

And that, my friends, is why marketing for advisors is an anomaly and requires a totally different approach.

The natural process most people go through to find an advisor begins with asking for referrals, and that's why your marketing approach should be centered on referrals as well, not marketing to get the attention of strangers. In other words, the goal of your marketing isn't to create a new stream of prospects *in addition* to your referrals. It's to turn your existing stream of referrals into a river. Simply put, if you want to grow your financial practice, you have to become a Referral Magnet, and I'm going to show you how.

MY STORY

I'm one of those rare people who actually works in the industry I got a degree in. In fact, my lifelong love for marketing started when I was in high school. I needed an elective and thought marketing sounded interesting, and I've been hooked ever since. I've also always loved helping business owners succeed. Coming from a long line of them on both sides of my family, I have a deep appreciation for the courage, sacrifice, and hard work it takes to make it.

I've always been fascinated with consumer behavior and studying how and why people make certain buying decisions. When people think of marketing, they often think of snazzy ads and clever slogans, but marketing is so much more than that. At the core, it's all about telling the story of a business in a way that compels its target market to take action. You have to understand what consumers care about and what their decision-making process is like, and you have to know what's different and special about the business so you can highlight the right things in the right ways.

Over the years, I've done all kinds of marketing—huge international brands, tiny mom-and-pop shops, and everything in between. No matter the industry, I've always loved what I do, but when I started working with financial advisors in 2012, I fell in love in a whole different way and decided to focus solely on this industry moving forward.

WHY ON EARTH?

When I meet other marketing people at conferences and events and tell them what I do, they usually look at me like I'm crazy before asking, "Why on earth would you want to work in the financial sector?" They know the rules and restrictions and think it's crazy for someone to *want* to deal with all that. Heck, I even have financial advisors ask me why I would choose this niche. No, I'm not a glutton for punishment; the truth is, I've just always loved a good challenge, and helping advisors do great marketing despite all the obstacles is definitely a challenge.

Plus, I can truly relate to what advisors like you do. When your clients first come to you, they don't understand their financial situation or what they should be doing to maximize and protect their money. There are so many different options out there and so much bad advice floating around that it's hard to know what to do—and that's where you come in. You look at the big picture of where they are and where they're trying to go, and then you explain everything to them in a way that makes sense. You give them clarity to make the right decisions, and then you guide and support them along the way. You take them from a place of confusion where they're on the wrong path—or no path at all—and you get them on the right path.

And that's exactly what I do for advisors when it comes to their marketing.

WHAT YOU'LL LEARN FROM THIS BOOK

In this book, you will learn:

→   Why referrals will make or break your business
→   The common mistakes that drive referrals away
→   How to create a referable brand
→   How to appeal to your target market
→   How your staff impacts your referrals
→   Why your website is crucial and how to improve it
→   How to craft the right USP and elevator pitch
→   What social media strategies you should be using
→   How to boost your credibility and reputation
→   How to use client events to get more referrals
→   How to put it all together and become a Referral Magnet

You'll see that the book is divided into two parts: Part I is all about making yourself and your brand as referable as possible. The foundational principles in Chapters 1–5 are critical in order to become a Referral Magnet. In Part II, we'll dive into the active marketing and branding strategies you can implement in order to build stronger relationships with the people you know and drive more referrals to your practice.

As we go, I'll use real-life examples from some of my most successful clients to teach you what other people in the industry are doing. You will also see links to additional resources throughout the book where you can go online and download free tools to help you implement what you learn and become the Referral Magnet you were meant to be.

MY HEART FOR YOUR BUSINESS

There's one more reason why I wrote this book and why I want to help financial advisors reach more people.

In 2006, my mom was diagnosed with early-onset dementia. It was the kind that affected her personality, behavior, and decision-making ability before it affected her memory. When someone can't remember things, you can tell something is wrong. But when someone's behavior just becomes strange, you don't always realize what's going on. We didn't know that she was sick until it was too late.

My mom was a business owner her whole life, a speech pathologist with a successful practice. She had saved up a nice nest egg to take care of herself. But shortly before we figured out that she was sick and needed help managing her affairs, she gave away her entire life savings to a televangelist. We fought to get it back, but there was nothing we could do.

The one saving grace we had as a family is that my mom had bought a long-term care policy a year before she got sick—a recommendation from her financial advisor. That policy was our family's salvation as we took care of her for the next ten years until she passed away. I can't even imagine what we would have done without it. I was in my twenties, my husband and I had just had our first child, and we didn't have a lot of money; there's no way we could have afforded to pay for all of her care on our own.

Because she had purchased that policy, however, she was able to have great care the rest of her life, and we had peace of mind. She also had life insurance, again thanks to her financial advisor, and that was a blessing to our family when she passed away in 2015.

Toward the end of my mom's journey, my dad was diagnosed with stage-four cancer, and his situation was a stark contrast to my mom's. He didn't have a financial advisor, hadn't saved for retirement, and he didn't have life, disability, or long-term care insurance. Sick from his chemo and radiation treatments, he was still trying to work and earn a living from his hospital bed right up to the end. When he passed in 2019, there was no life insurance and his estate is something we were still sorting through more than a year later.

Going through all of that with both of my parents has given me an even greater appreciation for what you do as a financial advisor. You make a huge difference in people's lives by protecting them and the people they care about. You prepare them for the future no matter what life throws their way. And while you're out there helping others, my hope is to give something back to you by teaching you how to reach more families through the people you already know.

Are you ready?

Let's get started.

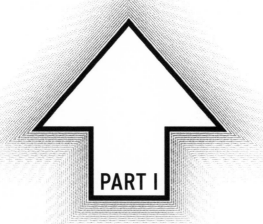

BUILDING A
REFERABLE BRAND

CHAPTER 1

REFERRALS WILL MAKE OR BREAK YOUR BUSINESS

Several years ago, I spoke at a conference for financial advisors about the power of your web presence and how it's either helping or hurting your business, whether you realize it or not. When I was done speaking, an advisor named Lou came up to tell me that he enjoyed my presentation, and although he didn't need my help personally, it was really interesting information.

"I've been in business for twenty-five years," Lou explained, "and I only work with referrals, so my web presence doesn't really matter. My clients are all ultra-high net worth, and they find me through my other clients or people I know in the community."

I asked Lou if he had a website, and he laughed and said, "Well, sure I do, but it's terrible so I don't send it to anyone. I haven't looked at it in years, and I honestly couldn't even tell you what's on there."

If I had a dime for every time I've heard that.

I explained to Lou the same thing I've explained to countless advisors over the years—that people *are* going to your website whether you're sending them there or not. That's normal consumer behavior. They get referred to you, they Google you to check you out, and then they make a decision about whether to contact you based on what they find.

Lou was skeptical, but he was horrified at the mere *possibility* of people going to his website. He may not have known what was on there, but he knew it wasn't a good first impression, so I asked if he wanted to check the analytics to see how many people had taken a look.

After making some calls and tracking down his password, we logged into the back end of his template website, and Lou was shocked and embarrassed by what we saw. I was right that people had been going to his website all along, and most of them were bouncing off in under a minute.

FUN FACT

My favorite definition of a "bounce" comes from a Google programmer who once said, "A bounce is a one-page website visit where someone arrives, throws up, and leaves."

Lou was an extremely impressive advisor serving extremely impressive clients, but his website didn't paint that picture at all. Instead, it was an archaic template with canned content that made no sense for his clientele. It talked about things like helping families save for college, which is obviously not a concern of the ultra-high-net-worth clients he serves, and it didn't talk about things like estate planning and philanthropy.

If I was ultra-high net worth and someone had referred me to Lou, I would have bounced off his website, too, because he looked like he specialized in selling insurance to middle-class families, not complex financial planning for wealthy families.

THE IMPORTANCE OF REFERRALS

Lou held the common misconception that because he receives referrals, that means he's *referable*. We'll talk about what being referable means—and what it looks like—throughout this book. For now, let's look at why referrals should be the foundation of your practice.

As I mentioned in the Introduction, when I start working with an advisor, one of the first things I ask them is where their new clients come from. More often than not, they'll tell me that most of their clients come from referrals or people they know in their personal lives, but they say it almost apologetically.

"I mostly just work with referrals. I know that's bad and I should be doing more marketing, but..."

Don't get me wrong, these advisors are grateful that they've grown over the years through referrals; it's just that they think they should be doing some kind of marketing or advertising as well and that referrals shouldn't be their primary source of new business. They think of referrals like the icing on the cake, but the truth is, referrals are the cake itself, and that's why marketing for advisors focuses on having your cake and eating it, too.

I can't say this enough: the financial services industry is a marketing anomaly. What works for other types of businesses isn't likely going to work for you, and that's why you have to take all the latest and greatest marketing trends with a grain of salt. Marketing is all about tapping into consumer behavior, and the consumer behavior of someone looking for an advisor is truly unique.

As consumers, we make our buying decisions different ways depending on what's at stake. Think about the different approaches you'd take in these scenarios:

→ Deciding where to take your spouse for dinner
→ Finding a real estate agent to sell your house
→ Choosing an oncologist to treat your cancer

Your approach with each of those buying decisions would be very different because of what's on the line, and that's why the marketing approaches of the restaurant, real estate agent, and oncologist have to be different as well.

With that in mind, think about what's at stake when someone is looking for a financial advisor. They're essentially looking for someone to keep them financially secure for the rest of their lives, someone who will look after their best interests and protect the people they care about most, and someone who knows how to help them maximize and protect every penny they've worked so hard to earn and save over the years.

It's a huge decision that is truly unlike any other, and that's why the first thing most people do when they're looking for a financial advisor is ask other people they know, like, and trust who they use.

Now are you starting to see why referrals are the cake, not the icing?

If you focus on growing your business through referrals instead of marketing to strangers, you'll be going *with* the grain of consumer behavior instead of *against* it.

Does that mean other types of marketing don't work at all? Of course not. The truth is, everything works to some extent in marketing, so it's about figuring out what works the best for the least amount of time, money, and effort. For advisors, that's referrals.

This is good news for several reasons. First and foremost, growing your business through referrals is enjoyable for most advisors. You're undoubtedly a relational person or you wouldn't be in this industry, and you truly care about the people you work with and know in your community. When you focus on growing your business by serving them on a higher level, it just feels good. As you'll learn in this book, all it takes to drastically impact the number of highly qualified referrals you're getting is implementing a few key strategies with intentionality. The end result is you making a greater impact on your community than ever before and impacting your own bottom line in the process.

Another great thing about focusing on growth through referrals is that it's easier than ever before, thanks to technology. We have incredible tools we can use to communicate and connect with people, form and strengthen bonds, and even get exposed to new networks of people, all with minimal time and effort on our part.

Before the internet era, the only way to really strengthen our relationships with people was by spending time with them in person or on the phone, but that's not the case anymore with the advent of tools like social media. If you find yourself with a couple of minutes to spare between meetings, you can jump on Facebook and comment on a client's post. When you do that, you begin to change your role in their life from just being their financial advisor to also being their friend, and people bend over backward to refer their friends.

Now don't get me wrong, the internet is not a replacement for direct human interaction and it never will be, but it is a new tool in your tool chest.

Finally, focusing on growth through referrals is great because it's something you can actually do despite all the restrictions and limitations on marketing in the financial sector. You don't have to jump on the bandwagon of every new social media site that starts trending or try to stay up to speed with what everybody else is doing. After all, you probably can't do what they're allowed to do anyway. Instead of constantly chasing a moving target like most businesses have to, you can focus on mastering a handful of referral-oriented tactics to grow your business in a way that is both enjoyable and incredibly effective.

Together, we'll explore those tactics throughout the rest of this book, and you'll walk away with a handful of rock-solid strategies you can start implementing right now in your practice to generate more referrals than ever before.

Before we begin, though, let me take a moment to dispel some of the most common myths and misconceptions I hear from advisors so we're all starting on the same page.

MYTH 1: FOCUSING ON REFERRALS ISN'T MARKETING

The most common myth I hear is that focusing on referrals somehow "doesn't count" as marketing.

Not true! Everything I'm going to teach you in this book is about using marketing, branding, and advertising techniques to get more referrals. This misconception here lies in how most people define those terms, so let me give you my definitions for them.

MARKETING

Marketing encompasses everything you do so that clients and prospects know, like, or think about you more. When you take a client to lunch or out for a round of golf, that's marketing. When you send a client a birthday card or post happy birthday on their Facebook wall, that's marketing, too. Anything you do that results in being top of mind and making people feel more connected to you is marketing.

BRANDING

Branding is creating a memorable representation of who you are.

Think about Apple for a second. What words come to mind? Most people will say things like simple, elegant, cutting edge, unique, and high end—and you can easily see those things in everything Apple does. From the sleekness of their products and packaging, to the look of their stores and how the employees interact with you, the Apple brand is incredibly well defined and woven into the customer experience at every turn.

ADVERTISING

Advertising involves spending money to promote yourself on a particular channel or platform. Advertising can be online, like boosting a Facebook post or optimizing your website to rank higher on Google, or it can be offline, like running a TV commercial or putting an ad in the local newspaper. Advertising costs money and involves someone else spreading a message for you in order to shine a spotlight on you.

The first part of this book will show you how to build a referable brand, and the second part will focus on the marketing and advertising techniques you can use to generate and convert referrals.

MYTH 2: IF I WANT TO GROW MY BUSINESS, I HAVE TO GO AFTER THE MASSES

Advisors love getting referrals because they're often presold and ready to convert into some kind of client relationship. But they mistakenly think they also have to market to the masses if they really want to grow.

Advisors tell me all the time, "There are millions of people in my target market who I'm not tapping into. *That's* who I need to reach!" Sometimes when I ask them who their target market is—who are the people you are specifically trying to reach?—their answer is, "Anyone who's breathing."

But as a financial advisor, your target market is not the masses. (We'll look more at who it *is* in chapter 3.) A lot of people confuse who their target market is with who they'd be willing to work with, and they think, "I'm willing to work with anybody, so I'm targeting everybody. My target market is the world!"

But that's not correct. "The masses" includes people who are too poor to do business with you. It includes people who are too young to do business with you, or who have no interest in managing their money, or who already have a financial advisor. So even if you're willing to work with anyone who has money and doesn't already have an advisor, that doesn't mean you should be marketing your message to the masses.

The other reason marketing to the masses isn't the right strategy for advisors is the uniqueness of the advisor-client relationship. Think about it. Each of your clients puts an incredible amount of trust in you to keep them financially secure for the rest of their lives. They trust that they're always going to be able to pay their bills, have a roof over their head, and maintain the standard of living they want now and throughout their retirement, no matter how long it lasts. They're relying on you right now to set them up for a secure future and maybe to even take care of future generations of their family.

For that reason, choosing a financial advisor is an enormous decision that people don't take lightly. Unfortunately, the industry sometimes gets a bad rap, and people are leery of choosing someone who's only going to care about the commission they're going to earn. They're afraid of being taken advantage of and making a mistake, and when they try to do their own research about financial products and solutions, they end up overwhelmed with the volume of conflicting advice.

At the end of the day, it's really hard for people to understand what all their options are, let alone make good decisions that are going to help them accomplish their goals, and that's why they need to find an advisor they can truly trust.

With so much on the line, most people find an advisor one of two ways. The first is reaching out to somebody they already know. Maybe they know you because your kids go to school together or you sit on the same nonprofit board. They know you as a person first, learn that you're a financial advisor, and eventually have a conversation with you about their needs. The other method is asking their friends and family, "Who do you use?"

Typically, however, people *don't* find you through mass media marketing.

MASS MEDIA MARKETING

Mass media marketing is exactly what it sounds like—marketing to the masses instead of to a particular segment. It has nothing to do with the people you know or who you're connected to; instead, it puts your message in front of a lot of strangers in hopes that some of them will bite.

Traditional mass media marketing vehicles are things like magazines, newspapers, television, radio, and billboards. These are sometimes called interruption marketing vehicles because they're designed to interrupt whatever someone is doing to try to get their attention. When you're driving down the highway, the billboards are trying to interrupt you for even a split second, just like a TV commercial interrupts you watching *Sunday Night Football* and a magazine ad interrupts you learning "Five Moves for Flatter Abs."

As a general rule, the smaller the decision, the better interruption marketing works. If a pizzeria has a billboard in the middle of town, it's designed to interrupt the people driving by, make them hungry, and get them to come in and buy some pizza. That's a great use of interruption marketing because pizza appeals to the masses and deciding to buy some is a very small decision.

In contrast, a billboard advertisement for a financial advisor is not going to work nearly as well. The people driving by are not necessarily ideal prospects, and with so much at stake, most are not going to be receptive to a marketing message from a stranger. Even if you come up with an incredibly clever and thought-provoking message that inspires them to get serious about planning for the future, odds are they're still going to call the guy they sit on the board with or ask their friends and family who they use.

Finding a financial advisor is a huge, once-in-a-lifetime decision, and most people are not going to hear a commercial or see a magazine ad from a stranger and think, "I need to call that guy and start planning my retirement."

That being said, it is a numbers game, so if you have a sizable marketing budget and can commit to mass media marketing for the long haul, you will get clients from it. Remember what I said earlier—everything in marketing works to a degree—but for financial advisors, marketing to the masses goes against normal consumer behavior instead of with it.

The vast majority of top financial advisors know this, and that's why they focus their marketing efforts on their own existing clients and centers of influence—not getting them to buy more policies or invest more money, although that's always nice, but strengthening the relationship for the sake of retention and referrals.

MYTH 3: GETTING REFERRALS IS A PASSIVE PROCESS

I talk to a lot of advisors, like Lou, who start out thinking they don't need to worry about marketing and branding since they work solely on referrals. Because they're getting a certain number of referrals, they think everything is working as it should and there's nothing they can do to impact the volume they get either way, except maybe asking for them. If they don't want to do that, they are passive bystanders in the entire process.

Part of the paradigm shift I want you to have is recognizing that you are already an active participant in how many referrals you're getting. The things you're doing in your business are impacting the number of referrals you're getting right now, so even if you're participating in a negative way, trust me, you're still participating.

You're a part of the process. You're either actively helping to increase your referrals or you're working against yourself by doing nothing. Choosing to do nothing is still a choice, but it's not the choice you want to make.

MYTH 4: IF I WANT MORE REFERRALS, I HAVE TO ASK FOR THEM

Have you ever had the unpleasant experience of awkwardly asking someone for referrals? Have you ever been on the receiving end of a question like, "Do you have any friends who might benefit from working with me?" That kind of question is uncomfortable for everybody involved, and it's not the only way to get more referrals.

You are neither a helpless bystander nor must you blatantly ask for referrals, which can be cringe-worthy and salesy. None of the strategies you're going to learn in this book will include asking your clients to send people your way. Instead, we'll focus on creating raving fans and inspiring referrals to come to you the natural way—the way people enjoy giving them.

That being said, I do work with advisors who have a specific way they've been asking for referrals for years with great success. If that's you, I give you props because that's not easy to do. I'm definitely not going to discourage you from doing something that's working, so consider everything else in this book to be a supplement to what you're already doing.

For the rest of us who would rather poke an eye out than ask for referrals, don't worry. You'll never have to do it again.

MYTH 5: I KNOW HOW MANY REFERRALS I GET

Most people think that the path of a referral goes like this:

> Sally: Hey, who do you use for a financial advisor?

> Bob: I use Joe Schmo. He's the greatest!

> And then Sally contacts Joe. Simple as that.

What *actually* happens is that Joe is referred to Sally, and then Sally will research Joe and decide if she's going to contact him. In other words, when someone is referred to you, their next step is not contacting you. First, they're going to do their due diligence and check you out, and if they like what they've found *and* they're impressed *and* you're saying all the right things and sending all the right messages, *then* they'll reach out and contact you. But most people never think about that process even though it's exactly the same process they use in similar situations.

When you think about it that way, you'll realize that you actually have no idea how many referrals you're getting. You only know how many are contacting you, and the difference can be staggering. What if you're actually getting three times the number of referrals you know about, but two-thirds of them are falling away before they ever contact you? And what if you could figure out why and fix it?

Game changer. And that's one of the things you're going to learn in this book—how to be referable and make sure you're not standing in the way of your own success.

MYTHS, BUSTED

Remember Lou, whose story opened this chapter? Well, after he realized how many people were visiting the website he was rightfully embarrassed to share, we worked together to build him a new one that was perfectly aligned to his high-net-worth clientele. Then we modernized and fine-tuned all of his marketing materials, positioning him as the elite agent he is—and his referrals went through the roof.

He's now such a believer in the power of his brand that he doesn't go more than a year without updating everything and continuously improving on it. He went from thinking his brand image didn't matter at all to being one of my most active clients who puts a lot of effort into the impression he makes.

This shift only occurred for Lou because he let go of the myths he had previously been clinging to about his business, how referable it was, and how many referrals he was actually getting.

CHAPTER SUMMARY

→   Referrals are not the icing on the cake for a financial advisor. They *are* the cake, and your marketing strategy should revolve around them.

→   When someone is referred to you, their next step is not contacting you. It's vetting you to decide if they're going to make contact.

→ You don't know how many referrals you get; you only know how many end up converting to prospects by contacting you.

→ Getting referrals is not a naturally occurring, passive process, and increasing your volume of referrals doesn't have to involve asking for them.

Now that you understand how important referrals are, let's dive into becoming more referable in the next chapter.

CHAPTER 2

BEING REFERABLE

My client Charlie became a financial advisor after a short career in the NFL. Many of his clients are professional athletes in the NFL, PGA, and other professional sports organizations. Charlie specialized in that niche because he understands and has a connection to that world—and he's had great success doing so.

Professional athletes have unique financial needs because they have extremely high incomes but for a very short period of time. Not only do they need someone they can trust with their money, but they also want someone who can handle the celebrity aspect, because there are a lot of people out there who want to take advantage of them.

Prior to working with us, Charlie had an embarrassingly bad web presence. He didn't do social media at all, not even LinkedIn, his logo looked like clipart, and his website looked like it had been built in 1990. Nothing about his brand looked like an elite financial advisor specializing in professional athletes.

Think about the message it would send if you were a real estate agent specializing in luxury properties, but you drove up to meet a new client in an old clunker. It would raise doubt about your own level of success, and your client would be left wondering if you understood their world at all. Would they still use you? Maybe. But would they refer their friends to you? Probably not.

Charlie was trying to tell his clients that he understands them, that he made millions in the NFL, just like them, and that he managed his money well and can help them do the same thing, but his bad website undermined his credibility. Right or wrong, people judged him and made generalizations that he didn't specialize in athletes, that he didn't care about his business, or that he was just old school and behind the times.

My experience with Charlie was similar to that with Lou (and a lot of other clients!)—he didn't really understand the role that his web presence was playing. An assistant had told him that he needed a website, Charlie said okay, and then he never paid attention to it again. Nothing on his website even spoke about the athlete market at all.

His assistant probably assumed what a lot of people do: that as long as you have a website, that's good enough. Absolutely wrong. A bad website is going to work against you every time because it actively turns off your target market.

It all came to a head when one of Charlie's top clients, a sports agent, leveled with him. "Your website is *bad*, man. I was going to refer someone to you, but you've got to get that fixed before I can."

Cue the phone call to me. "Can we fix this fast? I'll pay you whatever you need," Charlie begged. "I just need a new website by tomorrow!"

We couldn't build a proper website overnight, but we worked overtime and had it ready for him that week, and he got the referral. It ended up being one of his biggest clients to date, but that wasn't the most exciting part. Once he got his website fixed and then fine-tuned the rest of his brand and online presence, his referrals went through the roof—in part because his clients were no longer embarrassed to send their friends to him and because the referrals who checked him out were converting on a higher level and contacting him for a meeting.

Now that Charlie understands the power of his brand, his pendulum has swung in the other direction. In addition to his website, he hired us to build his social media profiles and design his logo and stationery. Like clockwork, he rebuilds his website every two years to make sure it's always cutting edge.

The same sports agent who was previously unwilling to refer clients to Charlie now sends him business regularly, along with Charlie's other connections.

FROM GETTING REFERRALS TO BEING REFERABLE

Lots of advisors have an embarrassingly bad web presence, just like Charlie, and they'll never know how many referrals they've missed out on because of it. Charlie was lucky that he had someone who was willing to speak that kind of truth to him, but most people won't—they'll just mind their own business and not refer people to you.

A long time ago, I had a housekeeper who was an incredibly nice person. She was someone I knew personally, I trusted her, and she did a great job cleaning my house. Despite that, I never referred her to my friends or family. Why? Because she was inconsistent.

She did great work, but every week or two, I would get a last-minute text asking, "Hey, can I move you to tomorrow?" Or, "Can I do your house on Friday?" Some weeks, she just didn't show up at all. I would come home and see that it wasn't done, and then I'd have to text her to ask if everything was okay.

She was great at the core function of what she did and she was a nice, trustworthy person, but she didn't deliver a consistent experience, so she wasn't referable.

Being referable means that you are somebody people are comfortable referring others to because they know you're not going to make them look bad. So let me ask you, how referable are *you*?

If you start trying to generate referrals before you're referable, you're going to end up frustrated, and that's why helping you build a referable brand is the starting point of this book.

There are two facets to becoming referable. Number one is having a brand that's impressive enough to refer, which can include things like having a polished website and a well-kept office that people enjoy coming to. Basically, you need to make sure nothing about you or your brand is embarrassing, so the clients you work with—and want to attract more of—are going to be comfortable and confident in you. When somebody refers you, you become an extension of them. Your client is sticking out their neck and saying, "I'm vouching for this person as my financial advisor." You become a reflection of their taste and judgment, so you want to make sure that who you are reflects well on the clients you work with.

The second facet of being referable has to do with how well you take care of your clients. I'm going to assume that you are a good financial advisor: you understand the job and you know how to work with money. But all the other things that go into taking care of clients—returning phone calls, availability for appointments, how accommodating you are—can also make you referable or not. Having a really nice website isn't enough if your client knows that you don't return phone calls or you're frustrating to work with. Again, that reflects poorly on you and on them when they refer someone to you.

If, for example, your client knows that no matter what, you're going to answer their calls or call them back on the same day, and you're going to give consistently great customer service, *and* you have a great website, then they're much more likely to send their friends to you because it's going to reflect positively on them.

Becoming referable may take time and effort, but it's not complicated. And once you do it, it's done. That pain point goes away forever.

In the next section, I'll walk you through the three aspects of a referable brand: visual, verbal, and experiential. When you make the decisions of who you are as a brand in these three areas, those decisions carry over to everything else. You'll have to update a few things as your business and technology change, but that's just maintenance, which is far easier than figuring out how to become more referable in the first place.

The initial work involved in becoming referable is not as overwhelming as you may think. In fact, you may not need a drastic overhaul of every aspect of your business; it's very likely that you just have a few things you need to fine-tune. Some people have an okay website but the wrong messaging, and others have the right messaging but wrong website. Some need to improve their client service procedures; others just need to add in a wow factor or two.

What we're going to focus on in the rest of this chapter is figuring out exactly where you are right now in terms of your referability. In other words, on the awesomeness scale of zero to 100, where are you? And how can you get all the way to 100?

WHAT YOUR CLIENTS SEE, HEAR, AND EXPERIENCE

Let's take a step back and take an honest look at your business. I want you to pretend that you are one of your own clients, and I want you to mentally walk through everything you see, hear, and experience as you interact with your company. Remember, every detail matters.

If you have a close, trusted friend who isn't already a client, you could have them go through the whole experience and report back their honest thoughts, but make sure they're willing to tell you the whole, hard truth.

YOUR VISUAL BRAND

The things people can see that relate to you and your company make up the visual aspect of your brand.

Start by Googling yourself, just like prospects do when they're referred to you, and look at what comes up and what doesn't. How visible are you on the first page? Do you dominate the results or are you barely there?

MARKETING HUMOR

Where's the best place to hide a dead body? The second page of Google.

Now go ahead and click on the results you find and ask yourself, "If I was a prospect, would I be impressed with this?"

Going through this process can be eye-opening, and auditing yourself visually doesn't stop with your online presence. Look at everything your clients and prospects see, from your letterhead to your office decor to how professionally your staff members dress.

Look at every single printed thing you use in your practice—slip sheets, informational brochures, even contracts and forms. They should all look like they were created at the same time with the same set of brand standards. Often, in a career that spans twenty, thirty, even fifty years, advisors end up with a slew of documents that were created at different times by different people. You want to make sure that everything looks unified with the same fonts, colors, and overall style.

Even the paperwork you give to clients makes a statement about you and your brand: are you giving them applications that look like they've been photocopied a million times, that are faded or crooked? Does everything have a unified look, or is it just haphazard?

Now let's look at your office. Is it clean, tidy, and well maintained? Do you have a professional environment that looks nice? If your client walks into an office that is sterile and undecorated—or worse, messy and cluttered—they make a snap judgment about you. If your office is chaotic and looks like you haven't updated it in a while, what message does that send about you and your attention to detail?

Don't forget that you are part of your visual brand as well. When you go to an Apple store, the employees there are wearing a simple, clean, modern, minimalist shirt that fits in with the rest of the brand. Your style is part of the brand in the same way.

If your practice is in the Iowa countryside and your clients are farmers, then you probably don't want to be wearing Armani suits to your meetings. Instead, a dressed-up version of boots and jeans is going to make you more relatable and approachable. On the flipside, if most of your clients are stockbrokers and attorneys who wear suits and ties every day, failing to do the same is going to make you come across as unprofessional.

This same principle also extends to everybody who works for you. If you have a professional and polished brand but your receptionist has purple hair, *I'm* not judging you, but your clients are. That's just the way it is.

YOUR VERBAL BRAND

The verbal aspect of your brand is comprised of everything you—or your marketing materials—say about you and your company. Just like how your visual brand includes everything people see, your verbal brand is everything they read or hear about you and your company.

The most important part of your verbal brand is your messaging: the content you have on your website, your headlines, your tagline, your bio, and the words you have in your brochures and other marketing collateral.

But the verbal aspect of your brand also extends to how you answer your phone and how you talk with your clients. What you say and how you say it are both important. What do people hear when they call your office? What does your voice mail sound like? What kinds of things do you talk about with your clients?

When somebody asks what you do for a living, do you stammer and say "uh" and "well" a lot? Or do you have a smooth elevator pitch that is short, sweet, direct, and clear? Do you have an air of superiority in your tone, or do you come across as humble and passionate about what you do? You may not have realized it until now, but your answer is often somebody's first impression of your brand.

We'll talk more about how to get the messaging aspect right in chapter 7.

YOUR EXPERIENTIAL BRAND

The experiential aspect of your brand is all about what your clients experience when they work with you. There can be some overlap with the visual and verbal aspects here because they are part of the experience. However, for the most part, this comes down to the kind of service your clients receive and how well they are treated by you and your team.

Your experiential brand includes things like how long it takes you to return calls and emails. Do you give proactive updates to people, or do they have to reach out to you and ask for statuses? Do you have a live person who answers your phone during business hours or a phone-tree directory that has to be navigated?

Think about your in-person client experience. Imagine walking into your own office for an appointment. What does it look like? Are you greeted by somebody at the front desk or do you walk into an empty space and have to awkwardly stand there waiting? Some of my clients have a welcome board in their lobby that greets whoever is coming in that day by name. In fact, my kids' dentist does that, too, and they love walking in and seeing their names on the board. "Look, they're waiting for me!"

Then think about how well you take care of your clients' needs while you're together. Do you schedule enough time for appointments, or are you always having to wrap things up before you're done? Do you ask a lot of questions and truly listen to the answers? What kind of drinks and snacks do you offer them? Years ago when I lived in Texas, I had a hairstylist who asked me what I like to drink the very first time I went to her. Every time I came in to see her after that, she always had my favorites there to offer me: black coffee, tea, and even wine if it was later in the day.

That's a relatively small gesture to make, but she made me a raving fan, and I was always excited to tell people about her.

All of these details work together to make your clients feel import-ant to you. I urge you to take the time to evaluate what kind of client experience you're providing and ask yourself *honestly* if you would be impressed. Your clients deserve a positive experience, one that is consistent and unified, and if you provide it, they will become raving fans.

TO THE NINES

Now I want you to look at each of the aspects of your brand—visual, verbal, and experiential—and ask yourself, "What can I do to take it to the nines?" Here are a few ideas:

→   Have a new-client questionnaire they can fill out to tell you what they like to drink, their favorite snacks, what restaurants they like, and so forth. I have a client who has a menu they send out before their first meeting with a new client that says, "We're so excited to have you in our office. We want to make sure we have the right choices on hand for you. Please fill this out and get it back to us." It lists twenty or so drink and snack choices that can be checked off, and she makes sure to have some of those things in the office whenever that client comes in for an appointment. It's a small touch, but it makes a big statement to her clients.

→   Use the same font, colors, and style on *everything*, whether it's your website, a brochure, a business card, or your new-client questionnaire. Everything your clients see should be polished and consistent.

→ Have a live person who always answers the phone during business hours. If you don't have a receptionist, there are services that can do it for you. Have them use a script so they answer the phone the same way every single time. Listen to what they say and make sure they do a good job, and if they don't—if they sound unprofessional or anything other than delighted to speak with your clients—correct them or hire somebody else.

→ When you can't have a live person answering your phone—outside of business hours, for example—make sure that your outgoing message is well thought out. Take it up a notch, and say something personal: "I hate that I missed your call. Your needs are very important to me, so please leave a message and I will get back to you by the end of the day." When you're unavailable, have a staff member check your messages and call people back to let them know when they can expect to hear back from you.

→ Do the same thing with emails. It's unrealistic to think we can be available to answer our phones and emails right away all the time, but you can have a staff person quickly respond to your clients' emails, saying something like, "I just wanted to let you know that Kelly's in a meeting. She gets out around two o'clock. I'll let her know that you emailed, and she'll get back to you then. In the meantime, is there anything I can help you with?"

→ Have a system for inputting personal notes that come from your conversations and meetings with clients. If they mention they're going to Hawaii, make a note so you can remember to ask them about it the next time you talk. Did they mention their love for the Dallas Cowboys? Jot that down and send them a congratulations email when they win a big game.

Those are just a few ideas of things you could do to build a referable brand. Now let's look at an advisor I work with who does absolutely everything to the nines.

A PERFECT EXAMPLE

My client Meg owns a boutique family office that specializes in financial planning for high-net-worth business owners and physicians. Meg is the epitome of an advisor who goes all out with everything she does, and as you'll see, it has paid off big time for her.

If you were referred to Meg, you'd probably go online to check her out, and you would be able to find her very easily because her web presence is search engine optimized. On page one of Google, you'd find her website, her social media profiles, and a variety of press releases and articles that have been written about her.

When you went to her website, you'd see that it's modern, easy to use, and updated often. Meg rebuilds it every year to keep it looking current, and every word has been carefully crafted with her clientele in mind. She's invested the time and energy—and brought in experts—to bring her vision to life, and it's designed to impress her exact target market.

If you submitted a contact form on her website, you'd get a response within the hour because she has her email monitored by staff members all the time. If you called the office, you'd be greeted by someone who is well-spoken and motivated to help.

Meg is able to lean on her team like that because she is very intentional with hiring. She understands that her staff members are the face of the company, and they're often the people who talk to her clients the most. She hires high-quality people, and she pays them well. She doesn't go cheap because she knows that if she wants the best, she's going to have to pay a little more to get it. She also knows that by compensating people well and giving them a good work environment, she can expect a little more out of them. They don't begrudge being asked to dress professionally and have tastefully-done hair and makeup; it's part of the job. They are a reflection of her, and she needs them to look their best. If somebody has a tendency to drop balls or not own their mistakes, they won't last long because Meg has a hire-slow, fire-fast mentality.

If you wanted to work with Meg, before your first meeting, you would receive a FedEx package with a document of things to think about, suggestions of paperwork to bring, and a warm handwritten note telling you how excited she is to meet with you. When you arrive for that first appointment, you'd find a beautiful office that always looks fantastic and is decorated in the same color palette as her well-defined brand. You'd be greeted by someone who was expecting you, and there wouldn't be any other clients in the office for the duration of your appointment.

Meg would greet you with a hug—she has an incredibly friendly and warm personality—and she wouldn't bring a cell phone or any other distractions into the room. You'd be offered drinks and snacks, and she'd make sure that she always has just about any-thing anyone could want on hand, whether it's coffee, a cocktail, or something to eat.

Every piece of paper she puts in front of you—whether a contract or a capabilities piece—would be branded and have a unified look.

As you talked to Meg, she would be taking meticulous mental notes about what you like and don't like—that you're a Dallas Cowboys fan and your daughter does ballet, for example—so she can bring them up conversationally later. She also has that infor-mation ready if she wants to send you a gift on a special occasion.

If you decided to hire her as your advisor, she'd send you a wel-come box of branded goodies like a journal, a coffee mug, and a thumb drive full of documents to have on hand. The packag-ing, inspired by Apple, would be high-end and fun to unbox, and everything in it would be beautifully wrapped.

As time goes on, when Meg tells you she's going to do something by a certain day and time, it will always be done by then or sooner. If you ever need something from her, even if it doesn't fall in the scope of what you pay her to do, she's going to do it.

I was at her office a couple of months ago when one of her cli-ents, a doctor, was purchasing a piece of real estate. He was stuck in surgery and couldn't make it to the title company, so Meg gladly jumped in her car, picked up the contract, and drove it to the hospital where he works. She's *always* willing to go above and beyond like that, and she's there to serve in any way that she can.

Again, every detail matters to Meg, and she wants to be known for excellence, so that's what she delivers—on all levels.

And when her clients are asked, "Do you have a financial advisor?" they don't think twice about referring her because they know she will deliver a consistently outstanding experience every time. They're comfortable referring her to their parents, their best friends, even their bosses, because they know they'll be in good hands.

CONSISTENCY IS KEY

As you could probably glean from our experience walking through Meg's ultra-referable brand, consistency is key. When it comes to your brand, you don't want to be like a box of chocolates, where you never know what you're going to get.

You want to be as consistent as Meg, and if you're not—if sometimes you email clients back quickly but other times it takes a long time or you drop the ball completely—then you may be great at what you do, but clients are going to be less likely to refer you to their friends and loved ones.

As a financial advisor, there are a lot of moving parts to what you do, and every moving part is an opportunity to drop a ball.

The things you deal with are absolutely critical in people's lives. They *matter*. The details matter, and being able to execute with perfection matters, too. Good enough *isn't* good enough—it's got to be perfect. People need to know what they're going to get from you, and they need to know that you're going to deliver that experience every time.

If you don't deliver a consistent experience, then what do your clients have to rave about?

Your clients refer you not only because of your ability as a phenomenal financial advisor but also because of how well you take care of them and how consistently you take care of them. When you wow them and deliver an impressive experience, *that's* what creates raving fans.

Occasionally, I come across an advisor who does not get referrals, so they have to grow their clientele through other means. Sometimes it's because they're brand new in business, and they don't have many clients yet. If you're in that boat, kudos to you for reading this book because it's going to help you do things the right way from the start.

If you've been in business awhile, though, and you're not getting referrals regularly, then it's probably because you're not creating raving fans. If your clients continue to work with you but they're not sending referrals, it usually means they trust you with their money and think you're a good advisor, but there's something wrong. Maybe you're too abrasive. Maybe you don't follow up or return calls quickly enough. Something is making them not comfortable sending people to you, and one way or another, you have to figure out what it is.

DETAILS MATTER

Why is it so important to be referable? Well, let's look at a recent experience I had with an eye toward these details.

A friend of mine joined a country club in her hometown because her husband loves to golf, and when I was visiting her, she took me there for dinner. Their membership was brand new, and she hadn't been there for dinner yet, so we were excited to check it out.

Looking at the big things, the food was great, the wine list was impressive, and it was a beautiful space to dine in. They got those things right, but when it came down to the rest of the details, there was much to be desired.

For starters, when we walked in, there was no one around to greet us, and we had no idea where we were supposed to go. There were several different dining areas with multiple entrances and exits, so it was pretty confusing.

Eventually, a server saw us, and we explained that it was our first time there. She didn't welcome us or walk us through or anything. Instead, she just said, "Okay, you can sit anywhere you want."

"Are all the rooms open?" we asked.

"Yup," she replied, and we sat ourselves.

Later that night, we found out that each of the three areas actually has a different dress code and that we weren't technically dressed for the room we were in. That was an important detail not to mention!

There was no music playing, so it was really quiet. When we asked why, they said that many of their members are older and hard of hearing and complained about the music, so they don't play it anymore. I guess that's a viable strategy if you're trying to attract only retirees with hearing loss, but otherwise, that's very shortsighted for a country club and makes for an awkward dining experience.

The worst part of the dinner was when I asked our server what was good. She looked at me with eyes widened and shook her head back and forth. "Don't make me say it," she pleaded. I pressed her a little, and she finally said, "I don't like anything."

I couldn't believe she said that, but she was young and I tried to give her the benefit of the doubt: maybe she was new and just didn't know what was good. But when I asked her how long she'd worked there, she said three years. Even if she didn't personally like the food, after three years, she had to know what items people ordered and enjoyed, so she definitely could have made recommendations.

My friend asked her, "What about the salmon?" and she said, "Yuck. It's really thick and I don't like it."

Her comments were really negative—and unprofessional—and the food was wonderful, by the way! (Even the salmon.) It was clear that the country club hadn't trained their staff, which is important because the staff is a reflection of the club itself.

After dinner, we went into the ladies' locker room—just to take a peek—and it was a very nice space with steam rooms, whirlpools, and these beautiful mahogany lockers. And then we looked up— and I kid you not—right on top of the lockers, they were storing what looked like old files! Are you kidding me? Get a storage unit!

All in all, the evening was great, the food was outstanding, and we had a wonderful time, but I wanted to share all of those little details with you because they matter a lot. The lesson is this: whether you're a house cleaner, a country club, or a financial advisor, you can execute the big things with perfection, but if the little details fall through the cracks, you'll hurt the overall experience.

CHAPTER SUMMARY

→ Your clients risk their own reputation when they refer you to their friends and family, so they need to be confident you'll make a great first impression.

→ Being referable isn't just about being a great advisor—it's about the entire client experience you provide.

→ To become a Referral Magnet, you have to pay attention to all three elements of your brand.

- Visual: Your office decor and cleanliness, your web and print materials, and even your attire send a message about your brand.
- Verbal: Everything you say on your website, social media, and even in person should create a cohesive message about your brand.
- Experiential: Doing business with you should be a consistent, enjoyable experience where every detail is attended to.

→ Consistency is key for maximum referability. If you deliver excellent service *most* of the time but not always, some of your clients will hesitate to refer you.

Now that you are ready to receive referrals, who are you setting yourself up to attract? Let's take a look. Chapter 3 is about identifying your target market.

CHAPTER 3

KNOW YOUR TARGET MARKET

One of my pet peeves is restaurants that serve unrelated types of foods. You know what I'm talking about—Mama's Café: Donuts, Sushi, Burritos, and More. When I see a place like that, it takes all the self-control I have to not go in and try to talk some sense into Mama.

Why does it bug me so much? Because I don't like to see businesses fail, and trying to be everything to everyone is usually a failing business strategy. It doesn't make you appeal to a greater volume of people; it just confuses people and dilutes the power of whatever your real specialty is.

If you're a sushi restaurant, own it! Be the most amazing sushi place in town; that's what people want when they're craving sushi. And when people want a donut, they want the best donut place in town. When they want a burrito, they want to go to the person who's all in on burritos all the time. They want the *best* burrito, and that comes from a burrito place—*not* a combo burrito-donut-sushi bar.

Remember that there's a cost of being a jack of all trades: it makes you a master of none.

PICK YOUR TARGET MARKET

That strange combo burrito-sushi-donut place has a diluted (and bizarre) message. Who did they have in mind when they came up with that restaurant? Who wants to smell sushi while they're eating a donut?

I can't answer that. What I *can* tell you is that the restaurant does not have a clearly defined target market, and that's a problem. They incorrectly thought if they offered only sushi, they'd have fewer patrons, and by offering burritos and donuts, they're expanding their customer base, but that's not how it works. When people want sushi, they want the place that lives, eats, and breathes sushi. When they want a burrito, they want the place that's been making Mama's famous burritos for generations. You get the point. Mama's Café would be far more successful if they defined a target market and did everything they could to appeal to them instead of trying to appeal to everyone in general.

Business owners, including financial advisors, tend to get confused about what it means to define a target market. They think that as soon as they define a particular target market, it means they're declaring to themselves and the world that they're not going to work with anyone outside that market.

That's simply not true! Defining a target market means that's who you specialize in serving, not that you're automatically turning everyone else away. It means that's who's in your mind when you're promoting your business and what you offer.

Take my agency for example. Our target market is financial advisors, but that doesn't mean we can't work with clients who aren't in that industry when they come our way. We get referred to all kinds of businesses, and our client roster includes everything from hospitals to churches to restaurant franchises and more. We have the ability to say yes to whatever clients we want, but all of our marketing and branding efforts are directed at our target market, and that's the approach you need to take, too.

HOW MANY IS TOO MANY?

"But, Kelly," you may be asking, "what if I have multiple target markets?"

You might expect me to say this is bad based on what I've shared so far in this chapter, but you actually *can* have more than one target market. Sometimes when I ask a client, "Who's your target market?" they'll say, "Oh, I don't really have one. I mean, I work with a lot of business owners, but I also work with a lot of retired people." Great! That means you have two target markets, and that's fine! You just can't have *infinite* target markets. Let me explain.

Imagine for a minute that you've been diagnosed with a serious heart condition, and you're researching doctors to treat it. You find a profile for a local doctor, and under specialties, he lists your condition only. That makes a strong statement about his expertise in helping people like you, doesn't it? But what if, instead, he had a short list of conditions he specializes in, including yours and a couple of others. Would you still feel confident that he has the expertise you need? I would, personally, but there's a threshold. If the list was twenty items long, all bets are off. I wouldn't care if my condition was on there or not because he clearly doesn't *truly* specialize in it.

As a financial advisor, you can easily market yourself as an expert in up to three markets, particularly if they are somewhat similar. If I'm a business owner who's referred to you, and I go to your website and see "proudly serving business owners, executives, and retirees since 1949," that's not alarming to me. Those three markets are related enough that we're not looking at a donut-sushi-burrito situation.

But what if you have two target markets and they're not at all similar, like farmers and physicians? Although it's true that they have very different financial needs, you can still target them both as long as you don't try to lump them together in your marketing and branding. For example, maybe when someone lands on your website, you have a split-screen homepage with buttons that say "Services for Farmers" and "Services for Physicians." Then once the person clicks, everything from that point forward is specific to them and their unique financial needs. Or better yet, maybe you have two separate websites, one for each target market.

ARE YOU SAYING I CAN'T BE A GENERALIST?

Maybe you're in a smaller community and you work with

everyone—young and old, working and retired, blue collar and white collar. Maybe you have inherited several books of business over the years and they represent a bunch of different markets. Or maybe you have a larger firm, and all of the advisors who work there specialize in different market segments. There's nothing wrong with any of these scenarios, and let me explain why.

First and foremost, if you're in a smaller community and you work with pretty much everyone in it, you're not a generalist; you're a specialist in your community. So rather than defining your target market by the industry or age of your clients, you're defining it by their location.

Beyond that, if you have a thriving practice that serves a wide variety of clientele, that's obviously a great thing. You should still define a target market, though, so that you have a filter to run your marketing, branding, and business decisions through. You need to be able to ask yourself, "Is this right for my target market?" And you can't do that if you don't have one.

THE MILLION-DOLLAR QUESTION

To figure out who your target market is, the question to ask yourself is not, "Who am I *willing* to work with?" It's, "Who do I *want* to work with?" To put it a different way, your target market is not who you would say yes to working with, but who you'd be most excited to say yes to. Then when you're making strategic decisions behind the scenes, you can be thinking about that target market and what will appeal to them, and that will help you make the right decisions.

Note that I didn't ask who you *do* work with, but instead, who you *want* to work with. That's because your target market should be future-focused, not past- or present-focused. It might be the same answer either way if you're already working with the kind of folks you want to be working with, but it doesn't have to be. Your target market is the type of client you want to be working with, even if they're not yet a large part of your business. If you're not sure who that is, ask yourself a few more simple questions.

WHO DO YOU ENJOY MOST?

Different client types have different financial needs that you may or may not enjoy. Take physicians for example. They have unique financial needs because they start their careers late and they tend to have a lot of debt, but they're also high-income earners and need a lot of insurance to protect themselves. Some advisors love working with physicians, and others hate it.

Business owners present different challenges. They often invest less in the stock market and more in their business, so as a financial advisor, that might not be good if investments are your thing. But if you really enjoy things insurance and asset protection, business owners can be a great fit.

So who do *you* enjoy working with most?

This point is really important because the more you enjoy what you do, the better you're going to be at it.

WHO HAVE YOU HAD SUCCESS WITH?

The next step is to look at the type of clients that you've found great success with already. You want a niche that's going to bring in referrals from your target market, so starting with who you're already helping in significant ways can be a great strategy.

If you're not sure who that is, I want you to go to your client database and pull the records of the twenty clients that you've made the biggest impact on. Think about the people who you've had the greatest success with, the ones you've either made the most money for or protected from the biggest catastrophes. Pull those records, and then on a sheet of paper, I want you to jot down a few things about each one:

1. Is the client a male, a female, or a couple?
2. What do/did they do for a living?
3. What age are they now?
4. What age were they when you first started working together?
5. Is there anything that makes their financial needs or situation unique?
6. What are their favorite hobbies or interests?

Once your list is compiled, I want you to look for patterns. What do multiple people have in common? Their age or stage of life? Their marital status? Their personal interests? Looking for the common threads in your greatest success stories can be very helpful in determining your target market.

You can also look at the referrals you're getting. Are they mostly business owners? Primarily retired people? Pay attention to that breakdown as well because it's a reflection of who your raving fans are and who they're sending your way.

WHAT ARE YOUR UNIQUE OPPORTUNITIES?

If you have a unique situation that allows you to rub shoulders with people in a specific segment, that might be a good target market to go after. Let's say, for example, that your spouse is an executive at a local hospital. That probably means you have a lot of physicians in your personal social circle, right? In fact, you might even have an opportunity to do financial seminars for doctors at the hospital. That's a foot in the door that is very difficult to get, so physicians might be worth considering as a target market.

Alternatively, maybe you sit on the board of a local nonprofit, and it just so happens that several other board members are business owners. That, too, may be a foot in the door worth pursuing. Or maybe your husband is a firefighter and you understand how to maximize his pension and retirement. Maybe that could be a niche market for you, so you can talk to his firehouse brothers and sisters.

Look at the connections you have in your life and ask yourself, where do you already have your foot in the door? Where do you already have relationships, trust, and credibility?

DON'T CHASE THE MONEY

Remember that scene from *Jerry Maguire* where Tom Cruise yells "Show me the money!" over and over again to a shirtless Cuba Gooding Jr.? Well, this isn't Jerry Maguire, I'm not Tom Cruise, and chasing the money alone is not the right approach to determining your target market. Of course the potential to make a good living is important, but you can do that with almost any target market.

One of my extremely successful clients—top of his game, nice seven-figure income—works almost exclusively with school-teachers and factory workers. They may not make a great living compared to a physician or C-suite executive, but in his state, they retire with huge pensions. He's an expert at what they need, and he's built a team that can help him deliver it. Although it's true that it may take the salary of ten of his clients to equal the net worth of one executive, he doesn't care because he loves who he works with. He understands his market. He's got a great foot in the door, and the clients just keep coming to him. He's built up a lot of trust over the years, and he has the team in place to deal with the fact that he serves a large volume of people.

The point is that you can do well with any niche; it doesn't matter where they are on the financial totem pole. If you were guaranteed to net $1 million next year working with any niche, who would you pick?

NOTHING IS CARVED IN STONE

One thing to remember is that your target market segments will be consistent in most cases, but they're not carved in stone. Your business can evolve and change over time, and it's okay for things to take off in a certain direction.

I talked to a client recently who lives in Georgia and targets business owners and executives. Because of the incentives, however, a lot of Hollywood action is moving to Georgia, and my client has found himself being introduced to a lot of actors and studio executives. Do we keep his marketing and branding focused only on business owners and executives? Of course not. The right approach is to tweak his branding to appeal to the new entertainment niche as well as his other markets.

HOW TO ALIGN YOURSELF WITH YOUR TARGET MARKETS *WITHOUT* TURNING OFF EVERYONE ELSE

I have a small number of clients who turn away all business that's not in their niche. They are all in on one segment, and they do so well with it that they don't care if they lose everyone else in the process. If that's you, then you don't have to worry about turning off people who are not in your target market, but for everyone else, listen up.

Once you know your target market segments, the name of the game is aligning your marketing and branding to them *without* alienating everyone else. Let me illustrate with an example.

My client Ron is a retirement planning specialist with an interesting book of business. About 40 percent of his clients are professional athletes, 40 percent are schoolteachers, and the other 20 percent don't fall into any specific category. They are young and old in a variety of different industries, and they don't have much in common other than they need help with their retirement.

If you go to Ron's website and read about his firm, you'll see that they specialize in three target markets: professional athletes, public school teachers, and business owners and professionals. Do you see the catch-all for the 20 percent? Almost everyone will identify as either owning a business or working in one, so "business owners and professionals" covers his bases. Another catch-all might be "individuals and families" or "retirees and working professionals."

When you list multiple markets, be intentional with putting the key markets closer to the front of the list and then end with the catch-all. For Ron, his biggest moneymaker is professional athletes, so he intentionally lists them first. Then he lists school-teachers, and finally he ends with the catch-all for everyone else. That strategy works well for a lot of advisors because it allows you to align yourself with your core markets while making sure you're not turning off everyone else.

WHEN TO GO ALL IN

Most advisors don't start out with a niche—they work with friends and family and then eventually their business starts to grow in one particular direction. When that begins to happen, the natural question is, "Should I go all in on this market?"

My client Jamie is a successful advisor who's been in the business since the early 2000s. Like most advisors, he worked with anyone and everyone he could in the beginning, and then his practice took a turn. Jamie got a client who was a physician, and that turned into a referral to another physician, and then another, and then another. Without intentionally setting out to do so, his business naturally grew to a point where he specialized in physicians.

At the point that I started working with him, his book of business was about 30 to 40 percent physicians and the rest was a mix of other clients, mostly business owners and affluent families. He said to me, "I love working with physicians, and I would love to eventually have a practice that's nothing but physician clients. But do I go all in on that? Do I start branding myself as "the financial advisor for physicians" on my website and everywhere else since that's where most of my new business comes from? Or is that dangerous because I still work with so many other people?"

At that time, with two-thirds of his clients not being physicians, we decided to take a split market approach instead of going all in on doctors. When you landed on his website back then, you saw two paths: "Click here if you're a physician" and "Click here if you're a business owner or family." Everybody fit into one of those two categories, and the strategy worked well.

Jamie's physician clients continued to grow, and about a year later, when his book of business was 60 to 70 percent physicians, he reached out again to ask if it was time to go all in. He was running into a problem where he felt like his business card—and maybe even his business name—should address his target market more. He wanted his brand to reflect his work with physicians, but he still wasn't ready or able to turn away the other markets.

The solution at that point was for Jamie to separate his practice into two sister companies, kind of like Old Navy and Banana Republic. Both entities had similar branding and overall messaging, but each was geared to their specific market. Jamie carried two different business cards and had two different brochures during this stage of his business. If he met a physician, they would get the card and brochure designed for physicians, and everyone else would get the other set.

That's a complicated strategy that I wouldn't recommend for everyone, but it made a lot of sense for Jamie. And it bought him time until he *was* ready to go all in, which happened a couple of years later.

At that point, his book of business was 90 percent physicians. Jamie was no longer worried about potentially turning somebody else off, so going all in was the natural next step.

Now, don't get me wrong, I'm not saying Jamie doesn't take non-physician clients anymore. He still does when he wants to; he just doesn't market to them. They come to him through referrals, and if a referral ends up getting turned off because they see that he specializes in physicians, he's okay with that; and *that's* the time when it's okay to go all in, when your business has hit a stride and can survive working with that niche and nothing but that niche.

If you're on the fence about going all in, you have to ask yourself, "Would it hurt my business if I lose those other people?" In Jamie's case, it was, "Would I be okay if everyone who's *not* a physician comes to my site and leaves without contacting me or becoming a client?"

If you're not okay with somebody outside your niche vetting you, seeing your specialty, and walking away, you shouldn't go all in yet.

CREATING AN AUDIENCE PERSONA

Once you're clear on your target market (or markets), you can create an audience persona to see the people in your market even more clearly.

Audience personas are fictitious characters that represent your target market segments. They are commonly used by big brands to help guide strategic marketing decisions, but their application is just as relevant for individual advisors and small financial firms. When you create an audience persona, you're creating a filter through which you can run all of your marketing decisions moving forward.

The idea is that instead of having to think about a group of unspecified people, you can think about one specific person who represents the group. If your target market is physicians and you're creating a new website, instead of asking yourself if the website appeals to physicians as a whole, you can think about your persona and ask if it would appeal to your fictitious audience persona, Dr. Jones.

If this concept is new to you, you're probably wondering why you can't just use a real client as an example instead of a made-up one. The reason is bias. If you try to use a client who you have real history with, you will take into account their specific likes, dislikes, demeanor, and attitude, but that's not the point of this exercise. The point is to figure out what appeals to your target market at large, not one specific person, and that's best done with an audience persona—someone you know the right amount of information about, no more and no less.

Audience personas are so detailed because the point is to create a complete person in your mind but without the inherent biases of an actual person. Without a lot of detail, you'd just be imagining a person in a foggy, one-dimensional way, and that's hard to wrap your brain around.

When you do have a detailed, specific persona in mind, however, it's easy to determine if something will appeal to your target market because you simply have to ask, "Would this appeal to George?" George—or whoever your persona is—will become like a real person to you over time, and since he was developed by thinking about common qualities in your actual clients, he will be a good representation of them.

Maybe George is very busy, works long hours, and doesn't have a lot of free time. Well, when you're working on your website content, you're going to think about appealing to George and you're going to be brief because you know he'd never take the time to read a lot of content.

Going through the exercise of creating an audience persona for your business is worth the twenty to thirty minutes it'll take you to create it. It's a very powerful asset that will help you in a filtering capacity to make better marketing and branding decisions moving forward.

If you have multiple target markets, you'll need multiple audience personas. You don't want to create one persona if you target both business owners and teachers, for example, because otherwise you'll be making decisions that are in alignment with only one segment. Instead, you want to go through the exercise and create a separate persona for each of your defined target markets so you can ask yourself, "Will this appeal to Steve? What about Judy?"

As you're going through the process of creating marketing and branding collateral and running it through the filter of whether it appeals to your target market, you're making strategic decisions. You're thinking of how to frame information about yourself and your business so that it can be appealing and engaging for those specific people.

CHAPTER SUMMARY

→ Defining specific target markets does not mean you're excluding everyone else—it just means you have given thought to who you serve best.

→ You define your target markets by who you're most excited to work with, not who you're *willing* to work with or currently do business with.

→ Target markets can change over time according to your opportunities, location, connections, or experience.

→ To decide if you should go all in on one niche, ask yourself if you'd be okay turning away everyone else. If the answer is yes, go for it.

→ An audience persona is a great filter to help you make marketing and branding decisions without the bias of an actual client's preferences.

The whole goal of this book is to help you get more referrals and to help more of those referrals convert into clients. Fine-tuning your brand so that it appeals to your target market can help you do both, and we'll look at how in the next chapter.

CHAPTER 4

BUILDING YOUR BRAND

There are certain brands that are instantly recognizable. When you hear their names, you immediately have a picture in your head—like Apple, for example.

As a brand, Apple knows exactly who they are and what image they're trying to portray. Every time you encounter anything related to Apple, it's going to be a consistent and well-thought-out experience.

When you look at Apple's website, for example, it's intentionally very minimalist. The product is big and bold, front and center, with very little information around it. It looks sleek, modern, and focused.

When you buy an Apple product, it arrives in a high-quality, beautiful white box with an understated logo on it, and unboxing it is oddly satisfying. The sound the box makes when it opens, the way everything is tucked snuggly into perfectly sized sections—it's all part of a very well-planned experience.

When you go into an Apple store, it is also sleek, minimal, and modern. That's their brand, and it's carried through everything they do, every customer encounter. It doesn't change with different eras and different segments of the business—that's their brand, period, and that's what makes the Apple brand so memorable.

> **PERFECT EXAMPLE**
>
> Southwest Airlines is another big brand that is well defined. They've worked hard over the years to have a consistent image portraying value, lightheartedness, and fun. Their culture is friendlier and more laid-back than most airlines, so they have a bright and cheery look that's consistent in every marketing message they put out there. Their logo even has a heart in it to signify their focus on loving their customers.

WHAT DO YOU WANT TO BE KNOWN FOR?

As business owners, we should all strive to create the kind of rock-solid, memorable branding that Apple and Southwest Airlines have mastered. With intentionality, they have decided what they want to be known for and have shaped every customer experience so that the right messages are crystallized in people's minds.

Have you ever asked yourself what you want to be known for? When I start working with a new advisor, one of the first questions I ask is this: "If I asked your clients why they work with you, what do you hope they would say?" What I'm getting at with that question is what they want to be known for. Is it for being very proactive and great at following through? Is it for truly caring about their clients and putting their best interests above all else? Is it for taking the time to thoroughly explain things to people so they can make well-informed decisions?

Without putting some thought into this question, it's like somebody hoping to land where they want to be in retirement—*without* doing the planning to ensure they're heading in the correct direction. You would never advise your clients to move forward without a goal; similarly, this is the point to set *your* goal. Ask yourself, "Where do I want to be in the future, and how am I going to get there?"

Amazing brands don't just happen any more than amazing retirement plans just spring up out of nowhere. Apple and Southwest didn't stumble upon their brand experiences. They are the result of intentional planning, of thinking about what they want to be known for. Central to any brand that has ever succeeded is the high-level process of determining their end goal and working backward from there.

This is your time for goal setting, and the rest of the book will help you operate toward that goal. However, in order to make the most progress, you will need to clearly define exactly what you want to be known for.

Every advisor has different strengths and different weaknesses, so it's important to recognize your strengths and play to them. You should make the things you're best at the centerpiece of your brand.

Let me go back to the airline industry for a minute. Have you ever flown on Virgin Atlantic? The experience is very chic at every step of the journey, starting with the gamified website you book the flight on, to the posh seating at the gates, to the unique design of the airplane cabins and the incredible in-flight food and drinks. You definitely pay more to fly on Virgin, but they do a wonderful job of making you feel like you've splurged on something great. Unlike Southwest, they're not trying to be known for things like value prices and a down-to-earth attitude. They're both great airlines with very strong brands, and they're sending the right messages to their respective target markets.

So what messages are you sending, and are you sending them every step of the way? Let's start at the first encounter and see.

TO DBA OR NOT TO DBA?

The very first encounter most people have with your brand is learning the name of your business, either from you, from someone who is referring you, or from some sort of marketing message you've put out there. However people first hear about you, advisors have a business name that falls into one of three categories:

1. Co-branding with your broker—you don't have a company name; instead, your business is simply Jane Smith, Financial Advisor with ABC Broker
2. DBA using some variation of your own name—something like Smith Financial Solutions or Johnson Wealth Management
3. DBA using words that are meaningful but unrelated to your name—Alliance Wealth Advisors or Park City Investments

Most advisors start their careers co-branding with a broker. Many brokers require their advisors to start this way until they hit certain milestones; but even when they don't, it's often a good idea because rather than being an inexperienced advisor on your own, you can tie yourself to the name recognition and credibility of your broker.

At some point along the way, if the broker allows it, successful advisors often want to start promoting themselves as an independent company instead of promoting their broker relationship for a couple of different reasons. First and foremost, being known by your broker can be limiting. Maybe your broker is well known for their insurance products, but you want to be known as a holistic financial advisor, not an insurance salesperson. That's a very common reason for forming a DBA.

Another reason is control over the company's reputation. A lot of the people in your community already know your broker and have opinions about the company based on past encounters that have nothing to do with you. Maybe they have a friend or family member who had a bad experience with your broker and it tarnished their opinion of the company. The point is, you don't have any control over how good or bad of a job the other advisors with your broker do, so those bad feelings can transfer to you if you're co-branding with them.

The last reason that advisors want their own company name is to protect themselves in the event they want to leave their current broker in the future. Let's say you've spent years co-branding yourself with your broker, and suddenly things start to go downhill. What if your broker changes your commission structure or makes some bad PR moves? It's not impossible to leave and start over somewhere new, but it is a lot more complicated if you don't have your own brand that can go with you.

DO I HAVE TO HAVE MY OWN DBA TO SUCCEED?

Most advisors are best served by creating their own company for all the reasons mentioned above, but it's not the only way to succeed. It honestly depends on how stable and great your broker is and what kind of business you've created for yourself. There are definitely advisors out there who have built incredibly successful practices co-branding with their broker, but it only works if your broker is known for the same things you want to be known for.

I work with a lot of advisors from New York Life Insurance Company, for example, and they're one of the most impressive brokers out there. They've had a stellar reputation for more than 175 years, and they are widely known to have some of the best insurance products on the market. So if you're a New York Life agent and your practice is primarily insurance focused, there's no reason you can't successfully co-brand with them for your entire career.

However, let's say you're a New York Life agent, but you focus on investments and holistic planning rather than insurance. Is co-branding with an insurance company going to hurt you? It could because prospects who are looking for an investment advisor might write you off as an insurance agent before you ever get your foot in the door.

The reality is that there's not a one-size-fits-all approach when it comes to building a successful financial practice. If you're wondering if you should co-brand with your broker or form your own company, ask yourself these questions:

→ What is my broker's reputation?
→ Do I want to be known for the same thing my broker is known for?
→ How sure am I that I will stay with my broker for my entire career?

The answers to those questions should help you decide what's right for you.

WHAT'S IN A NAME?

If you've decided to create your own company, the next step is deciding whether to include your name as part of the business name or use some other meaningful word. Just like the decision to co-brand with your broker or form a DBA, there is not a one-size-fits-all naming approach that's right for everyone.

Sometimes advisors think that if they put their name on the company, it will be too limiting. They think that it will make them look small and unimpressive or that they won't be able to get other advisors to come work for them because their name won't be on the door, but that's not usually the case.

On the first point, you have to keep in mind that in your industry, people hire people. Even if you name your company ABC Financial, when people are referred to you or consider hiring you, it's usually all about you as a person, not the company. Naming your company after yourself, then, can be great for continuity and name recognition. Just think about the people who send referrals to you—do they refer your company or you? If you're like the vast majority of advisors, it's the latter, and that's why it's not going to hurt you to name your company after yourself.

When it comes to recruiting other advisors to work for your company, having your name on the door isn't usually a problem either, especially if you plan ahead and name the business according to what I call the law firm model. The law firm model pairs your last name with something implying other people are part of the firm, such as Group, Associates, or Partners. Other names can get added over time, creating continuity while the practice changes and grows. Smith and Associates can easily become Smith, Walker, & Associates. The Fullerton Financial Group can become the Fullerton & Jones Financial Group. The law firm model is something people already understand and are familiar with, and it works just as well for financial practices as it does for legal ones.

Is the law firm model or using your name right for everyone? Of course not. The most common reason I discourage it is when an advisor's last name is very hard to say or spell. In cases like that, if you still want to incorporate some kind of personal branding, consider initials or using some sort of family name that means something to you and can give you a story to tell prospects and clients.

I did a branding project with an advisor a few years ago who has a fourteen-letter last name, and she ended up using her mother's maiden name for her practice. Her mom passed away at a fairly young age without life insurance, and it was one of the reasons she ended up getting into the business in the first place, so she had a great story to tell when the subject came up.

NON-NAME NAMES

If using your own name isn't the route you want to go with your DBA, another option is to come up with a clever name that makes a statement about what you do, who you do it for, or where you do it. A few examples from some of my clients:

→ Premier Wealth Management
→ Physician's Wealth Advisors
→ Oakland Financial Group

These kinds of names are perfectly fine choices as long as they pass a couple of tests.

First of all, does anyone else in or near your market have a similar name? If so, don't do it because you're just going to end up confusing people and accidentally sending clients to each other for years to come. If another practice has a similar name but they're on the other side of the country, you're probably fine; however, if a lot of companies have something similar, stay away.

The second test is whether the name is easy to say and spell. I worked with a client who specialized in entrepreneurs and wanted to name his practice Entrepreneurial Wealth Management, but that definitely doesn't pass the test. Close your eyes and try to spell the word *entrepreneurial.*

Did you get it right? My point exactly. Plus, it's just too long, and that's not good either.

Once you decide on the right name, you can begin to build the foundational elements for your brand.

LAY THE GROUNDWORK

When it comes to branding, there are a few foundational elements that every financial practice has to have: a logo, business cards, letterhead, print collateral, and a website. We're going to talk extensively about websites in the second part of this book, so in the rest of this chapter, we're going to focus on the other components. Collectively, they are the groundwork for your brand.

LOGOS

Your logo is the heart of your brand's look, and it should not be clipart or something you create by yourself unless you have graphic design skills. It should be well thought out and designed by a professional. The colors and fonts you use will become the look of your brand; you'll use them repeatedly on your print and online collateral, swag, and maybe even in your office decor.

A great logo that adheres to best practices will meet the following criteria:

→ It should be an original design created just for you. This is your brand identity, and you don't want to share it with anyone else unless you are co-branding with your broker.
→ It should be flexible for use in different places and spaces. Think about most social media profiles and how the company logo has to fit inside of a square or a circle. If you have a logo that is very wide or very tall, that's not going to work. So you want to make sure it's adaptable. Oftentimes, a logo will have an icon or graphical element that can be used by itself in those scenarios; other times, a logo will have a horizontal version and a stacked version that can be used interchange-

ably. Either way is fine; just make sure you have a logo that's going to look good whether big or small, short or tall, wide or narrow.

→ It should be legible and graphically simple. It's okay for the logo to have meaning, like a compass because you guide people in the right direction, but don't get caught in the trap of overanalyzing the "meaning" of the graphical elements and trying to tell a story. You have a lot of opportunities to share your story, but your logo is the wrong place to try to convey it all.

To see what I mean, tell me which logo you think is better for Wauwatosa, Wisconsin—the one trying to convey eight or nine different features of the city or the simpler one that just shows a pretty scene?

I've never been to Wauwatosa, but the second logo makes me want to go there more than the first. (Although I must admit that the flying insects and spotted arrowhead are intriguing.)

Just remember, when it comes to your logo, you're better served by the same "less is more" approach used by some of the most recognizable brands on the planet:

Nike and Apple don't even have their name in their logo; but you see that swoosh, and you know it's Nike. We all know them because that's how iconic (yet simple) the logos are.

BUSINESS CARDS

"Can I get your card?"

If you're like most advisors, you probably love that question, and I promise you'll love it even more when you have an awesome business card to hand out.

Your business card is important because it's often the first visual encounter somebody has with your brand, and it's not the place to pinch pennies. I'm a big advocate of high-end, impressive business cards because they're not a huge expense and they are totally worth it. You can get a box of 1,000 ho-hum cards for $50, but for $150, you can get the kind of card that really makes an impression.

My business cards are very simple, but I have them printed on extra-thick cardstock with my logo in raised foil, and they make an impression and a statement about my agency. When I give one out, more often than not, the person I give it to will comment on how nice they are, and I know they've done their job at making the right first impression.

Here are three simple rules for your cards to make sure they're comment-worthy and impressive.

Rule 1: Minimize the information to maximize the design.

As an advisor, you have to have a lot of information on your card, such as disclaimers and licenses, and that means your cards are already going to be more cluttered than other industries, even if you use the backside as you should. You can combat this by asking yourself which nonrequired elements are necessary. In other words, do you really need your physical address on the card? Your fax number? Your Facebook URL?

The most important things you need to include on your card are your name and title, website URL, email address, phone number, and any required information such as your license numbers and disclaimer. If you can keep it to that, you'll be able to make the design look better.

Rule 2: Add a stand-out feature.

A typical business card is rectangular with flat text and images, so any design element that breaks out of that mold is a "stand-out feature," and you should have at least one. Good options for advisors include embossed or debossed logos, foil logos, or *slightly* different shapes or orientations of the card itself.

If you do want to alter the shape or orientation, the one thing to avoid is departing too far from the overall size of a business card. Wallets and business card holders are designed for a standard card, so if you create one that is too big or small or just doesn't fit, that's going to work against you. You can, however, do things like making them slightly smaller, rounding the corners, or printing vertically instead of horizontally on the card.

Rule 3: Print on high-end cardstock.

It costs a little more, but upgrading the cardstock makes a huge impact on how nice your business cards will look and feel. There are lots of different options to suit your style and preferences, including satin and gloss finishes and different textures and thicknesses, and many printers will send you sample packs of different cardstocks so you can see and feel the differences. Whatever you choose, just make sure it's not one of the three most typical cardstocks for business cards: 14- and 16-point cardstock and 100-pound cover stock.

LETTERHEAD

Another foundational element of your brand is well-designed letterhead. It's surprising to me how many advisors don't use letterhead in their practices and just print documents on blank paper, but that's a missed opportunity.

Think about writing a letter to a client and printing it on blank paper versus letterhead. Is the client going to look at the blank version and think, "Wow, she didn't even use letterhead. What kind of advisor is she?" No, of course not, nor would they look at the letterhead version and think, "Wow, she used letterhead! I'm impressed." The fact that you used letterhead is not something that will be consciously noticed, but it will make an immediate subconscious impression about the professionalism of your brand.

The key is to use your letterhead with every single thing you print for your clients, no matter how important or unimportant the document. The consistency is important here because it's part of your brand image.

Your letterhead should be professionally designed using the same fonts, colors, and overall styling of your business card. It can follow the same rule we talked about with business cards, leaving off any information that's not necessary, but because letterhead is so much bigger than a business card, you don't have to worry nearly as much about the space. Letterhead will typically contain your logo, address, contact information, and any required disclaimers and license information.

Some people also like to add their name and title to the letterhead and other design elements such as watermarks, abstract shapes, and pops of color. How simple or elaborate you make your letterhead design is a personal style choice, but make sure it coordinates with the overall look of your brand.

You can either have your letterhead professionally printed on blank paper, which you can then place it into your office printer to print on, or you can have a digital letterhead that you use when you're creating your documents to then print onto blank paper. It is a personal preference thing, but I recommend having both.

The professionally printed version can be on nicer paper, and the back of it can be designed with your logo or other graphical elements to make it even more special. You can print everything client-facing on it, or you can save it for the most important documents and use the digital version for everything else.

The digital version is also what you'll use when you're creating a document that you're going to email instead of print. You can save it as a template in Microsoft Word, and then every time you create a new document, you'll do it on the letterhead template instead of a plain blank document.

OTHER PRINT COLLATERAL

If you lay out every single piece of collateral you have, it should look like the same person designed all of it. Your folders, business cards, letterhead, slip sheets, brochures, envelopes, note cards, and so forth all should have one single, unified look.

So how do you make sure that everything looks the same, even if each item has been created at different times by different people?

The answer is to have a brand style guide used by you, your staff, and every vendor you work with. Your style guide identifies your fonts, color palette, photography and videography style, and any other design characteristics of your brand.

If you really want to be a branding superstar, you can even decorate your office in the same colors and style as the rest of your brand (just like an Apple store!). In the case of Meg, our example from chapter 2, her office is decorated in the same shades of gray and gold as everything else in her brand. It literally matches her stationery, her business cards, her website, and everything else she does, and I can promise you, it makes a huge impression.

BRANDING IN ACTION

I recently did an audit with an advisor who runs a very successful practice, having her walk me through her client experience and show me what she does when she's meeting with a prospect for the first time. After seating me in the conference room, she handed me a plain black folder and began to walk me through a series of documents inside.

When I opened the folder, every single piece of paper had a different look. Some of them were on ivory stationery; others were on plain white printer paper. Some had been printed professionally;

others had clearly been printed on the office printer. Some had headers; some didn't. The fonts were all different. In some places, she had an old logo that was blue and gold; in others, she had her new logo that was green and brown. There was nothing unified about it, and it was thoroughly unimpressive.

If I had been a real prospect, this would have been my first impression of her practice, and it wouldn't have been a good one. She would not have been polished and professional in my eyes, and I would have drawn the conclusion that details don't matter to her and she wasn't on top of her game. Again, this would have been a subconscious judgment, not a conscious one, but the end result would have been the same.

In contrast, imagine if everything had been a unified brand. Her folder would have been designed with her logo and her color palette, and every single page inside the folder would use the same fonts and the same colors as well. What kind of a message about her professionalism and attention to detail would that send? A much better one for sure.

CHAPTER SUMMARY

→ Build the foundation for an impressive brand by setting a standard for what you want to be known for and how you want to be perceived. This will influence all of your branding and messaging moving forward.

→ Your decision to form a DBA rather than co-branding with your broker depends on what services you want to be known for and whether that aligns with your broker's reputation. You should also consider your broker's overall reputation and how confident you are that you'll remain with them throughout your career.

→ A good logo is unique, simple, and works well in a variety of places and formats.

→ A high-end business card is a great statement piece and worth the extra cost.

→ Using professional letterhead in all your print and digital communication creates a polished and consistent brand experience.

→ Create a brand style guide to ensure each piece of collateral created for your brand has a cohesive look and feel.

Your company name, logo, and stationery are important parts of your brand, but don't lose sight of the fact that your brand is so much more than the visual representations of it. Your brand is not just you; it includes everyone who works with you, so you want them to be just as impressive as you are. Chapter 5 shows you how to hire the kind of rock stars who will help you impress your clients and increase your referrals.

CHAPTER 5

HIRE ROCK STAR TALENT

Have you ever gone to Disneyland or Disney World with your family? If so, you know that Disney takes a different angle on customer service.

First, the people who work at Disney parks are not staff or employees or team members; they are all called cast members. Whether a fry cook in a restaurant in Tomorrow Land, a ticket taker at the front gates, or the ride operator of the Matterhorn, everyone is cast in a role. And when these cast members come on property, they *know* that they are in character, which they cannot break, and their most important role is to do everything they can to deliver the most phenomenal experience to every guest who comes through those gates.

Disney is able to provide such exceptional customer service because they are very intentional and deliberate about who they hire. They have extremely high expectations, so they hire only the best people who can deliver at that level. It is a big deal to get a job at Disneyland or Disney World, as it should be.

The cast members who are chosen to work at the parks *are* Disney to the guests. The Disney experience is certainly not the corporate board members and executives; when you take your family to Disney World, you're not going to meet or talk to any of those people. Your entire experience with the brand is with their support staff—the cast members—and they have to deliver.

Why is this level of customer experience so important at the Disney parks? Even though some guests live locally or are able to visit every year, for most people, a trip to Disneyland or Disney World is a once-in-a-lifetime experience. Families save for years to be able to take that bucket list vacation with their children, so Disney provides an immersive experience that lives up to those dreams.

A-PLUS TALENT

This chapter is going to teach you to hire like Disney. Why? Because you—and even more importantly, your clients and prospects—are worth it and it will make a huge difference in the volume of referrals you get.

There is a point in most financial advisors' careers when things start to really take off. You find yourself incredibly busy, and it becomes difficult to juggle everything you have to manage. That's a dangerous place to be—you want to say yes to everything because you don't want to miss those opportunities or the money that comes along with them, but you don't have the bandwidth to deliver exceptional service.

When you're in that phase of your career, you need to invest in your own business. You need to hire support staff.

A high-level assistant is the best investment you can possibly make because they are going to alleviate administrative tasks from your schedule and allow you to focus on what *you* need to do to make your business the best it can be. But you don't want to hire just anybody. You want only the *best* employees in order to see that return on your investment.

Who you hire is vital because often the things that go wrong and contribute to a client's negative experience have nothing to do with you, the advisor; they have everything to do with your staff.

The people you hire in your office are a direct reflection of you. They, too, are part of your brand—the visual, verbal, and experiential, as we discussed in chapter 2.

Your staff members are often the very first contact somebody has with your office, whether over the phone or when they walk in the door. They take messages, return phone calls, schedule meetings, and usually they're the ones doing a lot of the ongoing follow-up work. Your support staff learns your clients' names and greets them warmly. They have documents printed out and ready ahead of meetings. They can help you modify the agenda from last time, have your presentation of services scrolling on a screen in the conference room, and ask your client if they'd like coffee or a Diet Coke when they arrive.

Well, they *should* do all of that. And if you've hired outstanding staff members, trained them well, and set the example of the behavior you expect, they will.

But if they're not high quality, polished, well-spoken, and reliable, they're going to make you look bad. When you hire someone who is rough around the edges, or who calls in sick a lot, or who drops balls and tries to hide their mistakes instead of owning them and learning from them, you can be the absolute best financial advisor in the world, but that person is going to ruin your referability.

Let's say that a client needs their life insurance premiums adjusted, so they call the office and speak to one of your staff members. Your staff takes down the request but then forgets or messes up part of the process. Whatever the reason, the adjustment never goes through. Is that your fault? No, not directly, right? But it is because that's *your* employee and at the end of the day, the buck stops with you. Sure, you could do all of these things yourself, but your staff is there so you can focus on being the best financial advisor possible.

The country club dinner story I told you earlier is another good example of client experience. What are the two core things that are most important? That the restaurant looks good and the food tastes great, right? The restaurant can get that totally right—they can have a beautiful restaurant and amazing food—but if the servers are rude and the hostess isn't helpful and there's lipstick on the wineglass, the experience is still ruined. You're not going to go back there, no matter how good the food is and no matter how great the owner is because you most likely didn't meet or interact with the owner. At best in this situation, you're not going to refer people. At worst, though, you're going to tell people what a bad experience you had.

You are the country club in this scenario, and your staff—like the waitstaff and hostess—should be an extension of you. Who you hire is an extension of you to the point that if *they* aren't good, *you* could lose business over it. If your staff doesn't return phone calls or takes a long time to reply to emails, they are driving people, particularly referrals, away.

When your staff *is* outstanding, however, they not only maximize your time, but they also make money for you. They're so excellent at what they do that it's going to help your practice, make you look good, and help you get more referrals.

That's important to point out because hiring is not the place to pinch pennies. You need A-plus people on your team, and typically, those people are going to cost more. Think of it as an investment in your business instead of trying to find ways to save money. From day one, hiring an A-level employee will bring returns on that investment. Again, you're worth it.

WHAT TO LOOK FOR

Hiring A-level talent isn't based solely on experience. It's entirely possible to find exceptional people who are just starting out. I have several A-level people on my staff who are fresh out of college, and they're phenomenal. Why? Because they *get it*. They are outstanding players because that's who they are. They have grown with the company and learned how to do their jobs amazingly well, but we were careful to hire only the right people for the job.

Specific duties and skills can be taught. Anyone can learn how to answer the phone or print a document. When you find the right people, they have the right inherent qualities to go above and beyond the basic job description.

A strong assistant for an advisor—which is usually the first hire you make—is going to be a right-hand person, someone to do everything you don't legally have to do. You want to look for somebody who is extremely attentive to detail, well organized, and able to prioritize appropriately because you're hiring them to juggle the balls you're not going to be juggling anymore so that you can focus on the highest and best use of your time.

They should have a warm, bubbly personality—I'm talking vibrant, bold, talkative, almost loud, vivacious person so that when your clients walk in the door, they will be greeted by someone who makes them feel warm and welcome.

This may sound shallow, but you want somebody who looks pulled together. It doesn't matter what they actually look like—young, old, thin, fat—but look for a person who cares about their appearance enough to present as polished and nicely put-together.

You want someone who communicates well with both you and your clients. If a client calls at eight in the morning but you don't get the message until three in the afternoon, that client has waited all day for your call. Your A-level hire should also have great spelling and grammar so that when they respond to client emails or do any client-facing correspondence, everything looks neat and professional.

Overall, you're looking for the person who simply *cares* about all of this. They go the extra mile because they care about your clients and care that you and your office look good.

That's outstanding talent.

HOW TO HIRE A-LEVEL TALENT

Because you need to find the right person, you should proceed very slowly in the hiring process—think weeks, not days. Every layer of what you do to recruit people should ensure that you're never going to accidentally hire anything less than an A-level employee.

I'd like to share with you the way I recruit new staff members at our agency (which, not coincidentally, is now also the way that a lot of our clients recruit their employees, too!). Since we started the business, we've had almost no turnover, so I think we've got a process that works.

FIRST, FIGURE OUT THE POSITION

Before you hire for any position, but especially for an assistant or office manager—someone who is going to take work off your plate—take the time to write down the details of the position. Try to include everything that person is going to need to do. Consider what aspects are important in order for that person to thrive in your company.

Most importantly, be real about your expectations and what it's like to work with you. Own your flaws—if you are difficult to work for, look for someone who can handle that. If you do employment testing (more on that in a minute!) and see someone who is afraid of conflict but you have a temper, that's not going to be a good fit for either of you. Make it clear what the position entails, the specific skills people need to have, and what kind of person is going to be a good fit in that role.

By figuring out what you need from applicants before you start the rest of the process, you are setting yourself *and* the person you ultimately hire up for success.

NEXT, RECRUIT THE RIGHT APPLICANTS

Although there are many sites specifically created around hiring—for example, Indeed or Monster.com—I haven't had much success posting on those sites, for my firm or our clients. When I run an ad, I specifically state *not* to apply through the site but to come to a specific URL where I've set up our hiring process. No matter how clearly I write the instructions, it doesn't matter—I inevitably receive dozens of résumés daily that come from people not reading the job description and just clicking a button to send their information. I don't even look at those résumés—if they don't bother to actually read the post, they're not right for the job.

Personally, I have had good luck by simply putting it out there that I'm hiring. I'll let my social circles know that we have a job available and ask if they know anybody who would be a good fit. Again, when someone is interested, I send them to our website so that all applicants go through the same funnel.

This tactic can also work well on social media. (In fact, about half of our new hires have come from Facebook!) I recommend posting on your personal page as well as your company's page, letting people know that your company is growing and asking if they know anyone who is interested in applying, then send them to apply at the specified link.

THE APPLICATION PROCESS

As I mentioned, everybody goes through the same funnel, which is a page on our website specifically for hiring. Anybody who applies outside of that portal is immediately disqualified. My dad, who was also a business owner, taught me this strategy. He used to say, "You have to let people disqualify themselves early, before they ever get in front of you, so you're not wasting your time." I've always heeded that advice.

Once applicants land on the recruiting page on our website, they are asked a series of long-form questions about why they want to work here and what they'll bring to the table. None of those questions are fluff; they are all there for a specific reason.

For example, one of the questions is, "Where do you see your career in five years?" With that question, I'm asking the applicant to explain their aspirations. If someone says, "Ideally, I'd like to own my own agency in the next five years," that's disqualifying. I'm not hiring someone to replace me—not out of feeling threatened but because that person isn't going to be satisfied being anything less than number one. Remember, I'm looking for people who want to retire with me.

Another question is, "Why do you want to work here?" With this question, I'm looking for what they know about our company. Have they done their homework? Additionally, is their answer all about what we can do for them, or do they also list what they're going to bring to the table and the difference they're going to make?

The form also has an option for them to upload a cover letter and résumé, but it's intentionally not required to submit the form.

Candidates disqualify themselves at this stage in several ways:

→ Using poor grammar, spelling, and/or punctuation
→ Not bothering to write very much
→ Not uploading a cover letter or résumé
→ Uploading a cover letter and résumé that's not customized to our company
→ Demonstrating that they don't know anything about our company

If they can't be bothered to answer the questions thoroughly, if they don't want the job enough to write a cover letter, or if they don't take a few minutes to research what we're about, that's not A-level talent. Honestly, we disqualify the vast majority of candidates here.

This isn't to be harsh; it's to weed out applicants who are simply not the right fit. You are looking for the person who is going to go above and beyond.

COME ON DOWN

Those who make it to the interview process go through at least three rounds of interviews with different high-level people—usually me, my husband, and a senior member of the applicant's department.

The three of us all have unique perspectives and look at people in different ways. I like to get people talking, to learn about them and their personality through what they say in a less-structured format. I can read people pretty well, so I get a lot out of just visiting with them. Coby will ask more specific questions such as, "Tell me about a time you were really proud about something you did at work." Or, "When have you made a big mistake, and how did you go about addressing it?" Someone from the applicant's department will typically use a mix of both approaches: chatting to get to know them and to get a feel for if they'll be a good fit in the department and asking specific questions related to the job.

All three of us should be unanimous that this person is great before they can advance to the next stage of the hiring process. We don't make the process easy because we really want to get a sense for who they are and what drives them in life and in their career, so we ask a lot of questions and spend at least an hour apiece with each candidate.

Frankly, when I'm hiring, I'm looking for someone who would approach the process the same way I would—the way I did, with the first agency I applied to. I bought two books about asking probing interview questions and practiced answering anything I thought they could throw at me. I bought a brand-new suit and drove to the office an hour early, waiting in my car until a respectable time, just to make sure I wouldn't run late. After the interview, I went back to my car, wrote out thank-you notes to everyone I had met, and had a courier deliver them the same day. I know that I went above and beyond every step along the way, and that's what I'm looking for here, too. (I got the job, by the way!)

TIME FOR A TEST

After the interviews, we have applicants do employment testing, something I strongly believe in. We use a service called Resource Associates, which has position-specific testing. If you're hiring an associate advisor, a receptionist, or an executive assistant, you can order aptitude and capability tests for all those roles and more. For a receptionist, for example, part of it will include a typing test, but they will also give the applicant tests to see how they think: "If you have these twenty-five things to do but you only have time to do twenty of them, how would you prioritize?"

These tests ask questions where the answers can't be faked. We've had people take them and received results like, "This person is smart and learns easily, but they don't take criticism well and they can be overly emotional." The results are really detailed like that, and in our experience, they're amazingly spot-on.

How much weight we give the test depends on what the position is and how well they did in the other interview phases, but it does factor pretty heavily in our decision-making process. We know that no one is perfect, so we'll overlook a few red flags if they are strong in other key areas, but too many areas of concern will definitely disqualify them.

CAN YOU DO THE WORK?

The last thing we do as part of the hiring process is give applicants test assignments. If you're hiring an associate advisor, you might give them a sample portfolio and ask, "What would you do differently?" Or if you're hiring a receptionist, you might say, "Here's an email a client sent, saying that they're angry and disappointed with the service they received. How would you respond?" Giving people real scenarios to solve lets them show you how they would handle certain scenarios they could conceivably face in the position.

I recommend having applicants complete the assignments in your office if at all possible. We used to send people home with the assignments or reach out to them after interviews to ask them to complete this last stage of the process, to ask them to provide writing samples so we could see how well they communicate. After all, being an account manager, project manager, or content developer requires also being a strong writer. We hired a few people who sent in outstanding writing samples, but when they started in the position, the quality was not the same. What we found is that when they performed the assignments at home, they were able to get help perfecting their writing—maybe their mom was a grammar teacher or they have a journalist friend. Whatever the case, the samples were not an accurate reflection of what they could actually do.

Having people complete the assignments in the office, however, ensures that they did all the work themselves, and it lets us know how long it took for them to complete it. If the assignment should have taken ten minutes but it takes them an hour to complete, that may be a red flag.

TRAINING

Even though A-level talent is able to hit the ground running and start making you money from day one, everyone needs to be trained to some extent.

If somebody has worked in the financial industry before, they're going to understand a lot more of what you're doing, and that's preferable when recruiting. But when you have someone great, don't pass them over simply because they don't have that experience.

In the beginning, I recommend setting aside a certain amount of time each day—it shouldn't take more than an hour—to give your new hire your undivided attention. During that time, you should be able to give them enough to do for the other seven hours. Then the next day, work on something else. The day after that, work on yet another area until you just don't need to give them that same level of oversight anymore.

It is a process, but spending one hour to get back seven from somebody else is a good return on your time investment. The tasks that initially take them seven hours to complete may take you only three hours, but the point is that *you don't have to do those tasks anymore.* You are investing one hour with your employee instead of spending three hours on tasks that you don't need to do. You're still saving two hours *and* you're investing in your future time.

It won't always take them seven hours to do what you can in three. Because they're A-level talent, they'll progress quickly, and eventually, they'll do in seven hours what it might take you ten hours to do because that's what they're best at.

Additionally, look at training your staff beyond just the specifics of the position; help them grow as people. One of my clients, Wes, has been doing something he calls "character development" with his staff for years, and we've started doing it at my agency as well.

Every week, we all read the same chapter of a book, listen to a specific podcast, or watch a video, and then we come together as a team to discuss it. One week, we might listen to a podcast about how to create better habits. The next, we might watch a video about getting better sleep. Right now, we're reading *Getting Things Done*, about how to prioritize better. The topics aren't usually related to what we do for a living; they're intended to help us grow as people, so it can be anything motivational, inspirational, or educational.

This experience has been game-changing. When we get together each week, we talk about major life changes. People cry. We all feel like we're feeding our souls with great information, and we're growing as a team.

In addition to training people in core job functions, exercises like this lead to lower turnover. People are happy here because we care about them *as people*. And when you treat your people well, it makes them want to do a good job for you, to shine brightly, and take great care of your clients.

SWING AND A MISS

But what happens when someone has made it through the interview process, they've been trained in their position and as people, but they still simply don't fit?

As you know, the buck stops with you. I'm in the same boat; I can't do everything, so I rely heavily on my staff to take amazing care of our clients. If my employees aren't living up to our standards, it hurts me dearly. And, honestly, it has happened—we've made bad hires that have made our company look bad. We've gone through bad seasons as an agency, from growing too fast and not having enough people, to having the wrong people, or the right people in the wrong positions.

As difficult as it may be, when you have a poor performer, you have to take action. It's never easy to take a job away from someone who made the commitment to come work for you, but when it's not working, you have to let them go.

My husband manages our staff, and when we have to let someone go, he looks at it as freeing up their future. They may not be a great fit at our agency or for what we need them to do, and *that's okay*. It's not about them or us; they're not bad people, and we love our culture, but it's not right for everyone. We're realistic about that. When we cut our losses and move on, we are able to find the right person for the job, and the original employee is able to find a job that's more in line with what they want to do or are better equipped for.

When you see the writing on the wall, it's important not to be in denial. Everybody deserves a chance or two, but if they're making critical mistakes, that needs to be addressed immediately. Write up the incident, saying exactly what happened and why it cannot happen again so they understand how serious it is and you protect yourself in case you need to let them go.

You get the credit for the experience people have with your brand, good or bad. If your employee makes a bad impression to clients, drops balls, or isn't taking amazing care of your clients and prospects, that finger points back at you and it's going to hurt your business and reduce your referrals. On the other hand, when your team delivers the Disney experience, that reflects on you as well.

MY DISNEY DAY

My husband and I recently took our kids to Disney World and had an amazing time. But there was one interaction that made the experience truly magical for me.

I have celiac disease, which means that I am extremely allergic to gluten. As you can imagine, that can make dining out a challenge. Often, the gluten-free option is a piece of fruit or a simple salad—no croutons, of course! I like salad just fine, but it can be disappointing when that's the only option when you're hungry after a long day of making memories.

Fortunately, Disney makes sure that every single restaurant at every park has a gluten-free option—not just fruit but a full meal. I ordered my food and let the server know that I have a gluten allergy. When the food came out, I noticed that one person brought out my husband's and kids' food, and another person delivered mine on its own tray. He set it in front of me, looked me in the eye, and said, "Ma'am, I prepared this for you myself, and it is safe for you to eat."

As somebody who gets extremely ill if I eat even a crumb of cross-contaminated gluten, I can't tell you what that level of reassurance meant to me. That remarkable touch, going above and beyond to serve you, is at the heart of every single cast member at Disney.

But honestly? I don't know that cast member's name. I wouldn't recommend that one individual or even necessarily that specific restaurant (though it was delicious!). Instead, I happily tell everyone I know, "Yes, it's absolutely worth it. You should go to Disney World. It's incredible!"

And remember, just as Disney gets the credit for their amazing cast members, so do you when you hire the right people in your financial practice. Especially as your practice continues to grow, your clients and prospects are going to increasingly interact with and be served by your staff members. If someone emails or calls because they were referred to you, it's likely that they will experience someone in your office before they ever get to meet you. That's why it's important to get it right. Don't wait too long to hire someone you need, and make sure the people you *do* hire are Disney caliber.

CHAPTER SUMMARY

→ Your team can make or break your brand; they are an extension of you and they are often the face of your company, so they need to be as excellent as you are.

→ Set expectations with new hires; be realistic about what it's like to work for you and what you need from them to make sure it's going to be a good fit.

→ Protect your time and help unqualified applicants eliminate themselves from your hiring pool by creating an application funnel that requires them to meet a standard of excellence before their résumé ever reaches your desk.

→ A-level employees might cost more, but they're worth the investment.

→ Don't throw new employees into the deep end alone. Take the time to train them, and it will pay off quickly if they're the right person for the job.

→ As callous as it sounds, hire slow and fire fast. Expect to spend at least a few weeks finding the right person, and free up their future as soon as you realize they're not going to work.

In Part I, we've looked at why referrals are so important and how to build a referable brand. In Part II, it's time to look at all the ways to market that brand. After all, once a client refers someone to you, the test starts. Will you pass?

PART II

PASSING THE TEST YOU DON'T KNOW YOU'RE TAKING

CHAPTER 6

RELATIONSHIP MARKETING 101

My client Gerardo came to me because he knew he needed a better website than the template one his broker issued him. He didn't have a big enough budget to hire us for any other marketing services, but he had saved enough money to get a site that was built just for him and geared specifically toward his target market. A website is often the best place for an advisor with a limited budget to start (and you'll soon learn why), and he was thrilled with the awesome site we built him. It was perfectly aligned to his target market, and every word on the site was strategically chosen to position him as a successful advisor specializing in high-net-worth business owners and physicians.

After a few months, Gerardo reached out to me again and said, "I don't know what the deal is. I keep getting comments from my friends and clients about how good my website looks, but my referrals haven't gone up at all. Nothing has really changed in my business."

Referrals usually spike after creating a custom website, so that was odd. We looked at his analytics and saw that his traffic and time on site had both increased a decent amount after he launched the new site, which meant he was getting more people on his site and they were staying longer, but none of that was resulting in more phone calls.

In exploring further, we looked at what links people were clicking on and discovered that the number one link being clicked was the one for LinkedIn, so I clicked on it, too. And what I saw was not pretty.

Gerardo's LinkedIn profile was not at all branded the same as his website. Instead of focusing on his successful company, his target market, the people he helps, and the good work he does, his entire LinkedIn profile was basically a giant disclaimer for his broker. It didn't even list him as the principal or founder of his own company! He looked like an entry-level life insurance salesman, not a successful advisor working with physicians and business owners.

He explained to me that when his broker first allowed agents to have LinkedIn profiles, that was the required format, so Gerardo had set it up thinking it was better than nothing. The problem is, he never went back to update it. He didn't know that the broker's rules had changed and that he was allowed to minimize the disclaimer and focus on himself and his DBA instead of the broker. It never occurred to him that his poorly branded LinkedIn profile was working against his brand-new website when it came to converting referrals.

Once we realized the problem, it was easy to solve: we brought his LinkedIn profile into alignment with his website and the rest of his brand. He even became more active on LinkedIn and Facebook. And as we expected, his referrals started to spike, and it was a happy ending.

MARKET YOURSELF

We've already discussed that when people are referred to you, their next step is not contacting you; it's vetting you to decide if they *should* contact you. They go online to check you out, and all the while, you don't know that it's happening. That's why I refer to the vetting process as the test you don't know you're taking.

> **BY THE WAY**
>
> It's worth noting that the vetting process isn't just for referrals. If you know someone in the community who's thinking about talking to you as an advisor, they're going to vet you before they reach out, just like a referral you've never met would. If you do some sort of advertising or PR campaign and capture someone's attention, they're going to vet you, too. Vetting is universal, and that's why it's so important that when someone wants to vet you, they can find you quickly and easily and what they find sends the right messages, inspiring them to get in touch.

When potential clients vet you, they're Googling you and, in most cases, checking out your website and social media profiles. They're reading your bio, learning about your education and credentials, noting what you say about yourself, and analyzing how legitimate you look.

But what are they looking *for*?

They're looking to see if you are the right fit for them. Can you help them? Are you good enough to meet their needs? Basically, they want to know that you're the best choice.

When it comes to referrals, they've already been told by someone they know and trust that they should work with you, so vetting you is a due diligence step. As they're going through the process, they're looking for things that either qualify or disqualify you in order to decide if they should reach out. So you have to make sure you have the right messaging and information or they're going to leave without you ever knowing they were there.

Imagine for a moment that I was referred to you by a friend who told me you're an elite advisor who specializes in exit planning for business owners. When I go to your website, I find an old-looking template website with a headline reading, "Specializing in Holistic Financial Solutions since 1953." As I continue skimming the home page, there's nothing on there about business owners or exit planning at all, and in less than thirty seconds, you have disqualified yourself. Why? Because there's a disconnect between what I expected to see and what I actually saw. Your website didn't look modern or professional: strike one. I'm not looking for holistic financial solutions; I'm looking for exit planning: strike two. And I see nothing about business owners: strike three, and you're out.

If, however, I had been greeted with a modern website and a headline that read, "Helping Business Owners Exit Their Business the Right Way since 1953," I would have continued exploring the website and been one step closer to reaching out.

A website visit from someone who is vetting you typically lasts two to three minutes unless they disqualify you sooner. People don't sit down and read websites front to back, top to bottom. They click around on the things they care about and skim the content looking for any red flags. That's why it's important to be strategic with not only what information you have on your website, but where it is and how it's organized. (More on that in chapters 7 and 8.)

When someone is on your website vetting you, you're not going to have a chance to explain yourself, to say, "I haven't updated this in a while" or, "This is actually what I do." They're going to look quickly, make a decision one way or another, and move on.

This vetting process is why customizing your web presence creates a big spike in referrals. Some of it may be because your website was so bad before that people weren't comfortable referring people to you, but most of the increase can be attributed to an improved conversion rate. In other words, you may be getting the same number of referrals, but you're not losing them when they vet you.

Always remember that you don't know how many referrals you get; you only know how many of them convert to prospects by deciding to reach out. In other words, you may average ten referrals a year, but what if you're *actually* getting twenty and the other half disqualified you during the vetting process?

"I DON'T WANT MORE CLIENTS"

...said no advisor ever. In my experience working with top advisors across the nation, even the most successful ones who make very nice seven-figure salaries still want more clients—and it's not out of greed.

It's because you want security for your family. You want to take care of the people you love and support the organizations that are dear to your heart. And you want to help more people the same way you've helped your existing clients.

Receiving more referrals—and getting more of them to convert to prospects—is the essential element to growing your practice and generating more revenue and everything that comes along with it: more freedom, more peace of mind, and the ability to live your best life by helping other people live theirs. If you get too many, that's a great problem to have because you can simply keep the ones you want and give the others to another advisor.

WALK BEFORE YOU RUN

The rest of this chapter is going to give you an overview of the most successful marketing strategies used by top advisors. We talked about them generally in Part I, but we're going to dive deep into the details in the chapters to come.

As we talk about different relationship marketing strategies, keep in mind that you don't have to do every single thing in order to increase your referrals. I want you to learn about all the different tactics and then pick and choose the ones that make the most sense for you. Obviously, the more that you do, the better your results will be, but if this is all new to you, I want to encourage you to walk before you run. Think about what resonates most with you, and remember that you have to be able to keep up with these techniques, so it's better to choose a few strategies that you will execute consistently rather than doing all of them halfway.

The only nonnegotiable is that you have to have a great website with custom-written verbiage geared to your target market. Without that, your efforts will never pay off fully because you're always going to lose people in the vetting process. I also highly recommend having a LinkedIn profile that has the same overall messaging as the website.

The right approach is to start with laying the foundation first: again, that's a website and ideally a LinkedIn profile, both of which are polished and tailored to you. Then pick one or two things you want to implement in terms of active relationship marketing. Focus on those first and build from there.

CORE MARKETING PRINCIPLES

I've had the unique privilege of helping hundreds of top financial advisors all over the country with their marketing and branding. Most of my clients are in the top 5 percent of the industry, or they're quickly on their way to that level of success, and I've been able to look at what they're already doing and build on it to help them take their business to the next level.

Throughout the rest of this book, I'm going to dive deep into the core strategies that have worked for them. But first, I'm going to start with a high-level overview of what they've done in order to become Referral Magnets.

1. CONSISTENT MESSAGING

Top advisors have messaging that is consistent on all platforms so that everything ties together nicely. That doesn't mean that you're using exactly the same words necessarily. For example, LinkedIn profiles are generally written in first person, whereas your website will most likely be in the third person. However, you want to present the same overall messaging with the same, unified look across all platforms. Why is that important? Research has shown that most people will go to at least a couple of different places to check you out and decide if they're going to get in touch. They're not just clicking the first link and calling you; they're going to vet you in several places first. Therefore, you have to make sure you're not sending any mixed signals like my example of Gerardo earlier. We'll cover consistent brand messaging in detail in the next chapter.

2. AWESOME WEB PRESENCE

They have a rock-solid, awesome web presence. They do not have old-looking websites with inaccurate verbiage on them. They understand that their website is the central hub of their brand and that everything else they do is designed to drive people there. Your business card lists your website. If you run an ad somewhere, it's going to list your website. Your social media profiles link to your website. Everything you do in marketing is designed to drive people to your website in order to convert them to prospects. It's the one place where you can tell your whole story: who you are, what you do, what your approach is, and who you work with. You can't do that on a Facebook profile or a newspaper ad; there's just not enough room and it's not the right format.

Remember that when people are making the hugely important

decision about who's going to keep them financially secure for the rest of their lives, they're not going to take it lightly. They're going to go online and vet you, and they expect to find you easily. You want to impress them with a modern website that looks good, has the right content with the correct messaging, and is well organized so people can find the information they're looking for.

Some people think that they can bypass this and just not have a website at all. After all, if a bad website works against you, you're better off just skipping it, right? Wrong! If someone is referred to you and they Google you and can't even find you, that's a giant red flag and it makes you look illegitimate. Everybody wonders about a business that doesn't have a website: "Are they shady? Is this really a good company?" It just looks unprofessional, so if you're in this boat and you justify it because you still get referrals, please understand that you don't know how many referrals you're missing out on because when they vet you, they can't find a website.

Not only that, but not having a website is a missed opportunity. People are looking for you, searching for your name or your company name, and the search engines are going to fill that page with something. If it's not your website or social media profiles, it's going to be something you don't control—somebody with a similar name or maybe even a competitor.

When you do have a clean, well-organized website that people can find quickly and easily, it can seal the deal and help motivate referrals to give you a call. We'll talk in depth about how to set up a winning website in chapter 8.

3. ACTIVE SOCIAL MEDIA

The most successful financial advisors also have an active social media presence according to whatever their compliance situation allows. No matter how you feel about social media in your personal life, from a marketing perspective, it's not a waste of time and it is a phenomenal way to generate referrals that convert. At a minimum, you should have a great LinkedIn profile because just like a website, it's expected and it's weird if you don't have one. If you don't want to be active on LinkedIn and post things there, you should at least have an awesome profile that contains the same company messaging as your website.

LinkedIn is also great because it ranks extremely well in search engines. When somebody is vetting you and searches for you online, your LinkedIn profile is going to show up toward the top of the results—in the first, second, or third position, depending on what other assets you have out there. It's a great way to help control the search engine results when people are vetting you.

Social media is also a great way to stay relationally connected to your clients and COIs. Because of the social media revolution, our society has a hunger to humanize business these days and get to know people on a more personal level. They want to see the people behind the business, so I always encourage my clients to "lift the veil" and let people get a peek into their world. Doing so makes them feel more connected to you, and over time, it turns your clients into friends, which results in increased loyalty and referrals.

We'll look at how to create an awesome profile—on LinkedIn, Facebook, and other social media platforms—as well as how to use social media actively if you choose to in chapter 9.

4. TARGETED RELATIONSHIP MARKETING

Successful advisors also do targeted relationship marketing to their existing clients. Whether it's sending out company newsletters, inviting clients for a round of golf, sending cards and gifts, or sharing a link to an inspirational TED Talk, these little touches are *all* marketing—and they're all important. Even more important? Creating a relationship marketing plan—writing down what you're going to do, putting it on your calendar, and planning the time to do everything—so you can actually get it done.

We'll look at ways to do relationship marketing with your existing clients in chapters 10 and 12.

5. COORDINATED BRAND

They make sure their brand is polished and coordinated online and offline, and they make sure people know it. They use testimonials if they're able to, as well as award marketing, press releases, and article marketing to boost their credibility in the eyes of their clients and prospects. That will be our topic of discussion for chapter 11.

6. SPEND TIME WHERE IDEAL CLIENTS ARE

They put themselves in situations where referrals are more likely to happen. For example, a lot of my clients sponsor and attend charity events where they're likely to be rubbing shoulders with ideal prospects. Their friends also attend, and they bring other friends my clients may not know. At that point, they're just one introduction away from a referral. Other clients have country club memberships and spend time golfing and hanging out at the club to get to know people. The point is to think about where your ideal clients might be and make sure you're there as well. We'll explore this and other in-person experiences in chapter 12.

7. THANK PEOPLE FOR SENDING REFERRALS

Finally, when a client does refer someone to a top advisor, they make sure to circle back to that client and let them know that the person they referred was taken care of. You want to thank people for sending referrals to you. Whether it's with a phone call, an email, or a card, show them your gratitude and keep them posted—even if it doesn't work out. It can be as simple as, "I just want to let you know that I met with Allison today. I don't think she's quite ready yet, but I really appreciated meeting her. She seems like a great person." Closing the loop makes sure that your client isn't left wondering if you took care of their friend or family member. That will give them confidence to send other people to you.

Embracing relationship marketing is vital to becoming a Referral Magnet. If you want to increase the number of referrals you're receiving and converting, then the information in the next few chapters is for you.

FREEBIE

As you go through the rest of this book, I want you to create your own relationship marketing plan so that you can walk away ready to implement everything you've learned. Download our free Relationship Marketing Plan template at TheReferralMagnet.com.

CHAPTER SUMMARY

→ "Passing the test you don't know you're taking" refers to winning the vetting game. When someone is referred to you, their next step is not contacting you; it's vetting you to decide if they want to. If they find you quickly and easily and what they learn impresses them enough to reach out, you've passed the test.

→ Implement one or two relationship marketing strategies that resonate with you the most, and then build from there. Don't try to do everything all at once or you'll end up overwhelmed.

→ Referral Magnets follow seven core marketing principles, which you'll learn about in the coming chapters:

- Have a consistent, unified brand message and style on all platforms.
- Maintain a well-organized and current website that encourages prospects to take action and contact you.
- Maintain an active social media presence.
- Participate in relationship marketing with your current clients through creative touchpoints.
- Boost credibility with press releases, testimonials, and reviews.
- Create opportunities to spend time with your clients and connect with new prospects.
- Show gratitude to clients who refer someone to you by keeping them in the loop and thanking them for the referral.

As we dive into the specific strategies in the chapters ahead, I want you to experience a paradigm shift—away from passively taking whatever referrals come your way and thinking there's not much you can do to impact the volume you get and toward actively marketing to receive and convert more referrals than ever before. It all centers on building and strengthening relationships, and that requires intentionality and proactive planning, starting with the first thing a referral reads when they vet you: your message.

CHAPTER 7

BRAND MESSAGING

Pop quiz! Who do these slogans belong to?

→ "Just do it."
→ "The happiest place on earth."
→ "You're in good hands."
→ "Finger lickin' good"
→ "The quicker picker-upper"
→ "When you care enough to send the very best"
→ "The breakfast of champions"
→ "The ultimate driving machine"
→ "Melts in your mouth, not in your hand"
→ "Because you're worth it"

Answer Key: Nike, Disney, Allstate, KFC, Bounty, Hallmark, Wheaties, BMW, M&Ms, L'Oréal

If you're a typical American adult, you probably knew at least seven or eight of these slogans, if not all ten, and that's because they are examples of some of the best branding campaigns of all time. They're catchy slogans, obviously, but they're so much more than that. Each of those companies offers an incredible product or service, just like you do, and they're using a carefully crafted set of words to highlight their unique benefit to consumers. When you pair a great company with the right messaging, the end result is a very powerful, memorable brand that resonates with the right target market segments.

SAY THE RIGHT THING

When people talk about building a website or designing a brochure, they tend to think about the design and content as being the same thing, but it's not. What it looks like and what it says are two completely separate things.

A great-looking website that says all the wrong things is better than a terrible-looking website that says all the wrong things just because in the initial snap second that the site loads, it's not going to give a bad impression. But as soon as somebody starts to read what you have to say, if the verbiage wasn't created with intentionality and geared toward your target audience, it's still going to fall flat.

The reality is that your brand messaging must be strong, accurate, and well written; otherwise, your referrals will fall apart at the conversion stage. Remember, you don't know how many referrals you actually get, only how many convert to prospects and reach out to you, so the conversion stage is just as important as getting the referral in the first place.

Imagine you're a business owner looking for somebody who

specializes in financial planning for business owners. You want somebody who *understands* business owners and the complex needs you have. So one day you mention to your friend that you're looking for a financial planner, and your friend says, "You should definitely contact Wes. He's really good."

Great! You have a referral. But then you go to Wes's website, and it doesn't say anything about business owners. Or it says something really small on a deep interior page, but the rest of the website talks about financial planning for young families. The first thing you're going to think is, "Oh, it doesn't look like he really specializes in business owners," and you're probably going to keep looking.

When referrals are checking you out, if what they read is not in alignment with what they were expecting or hoping for, you're going to be disqualified before you ever get a chance to talk to them.

One of the problems I often see with financial advisors is that they have a template website with template verbiage on it and they just use it as is. They think that just because they have a website and their bio and contact information is accurate, that's good enough. They assume that it's not going to work against them when it comes to converting referrals and other prospects, but that's just not true.

Even if your broker doesn't allow you to have a custom website and you have to use a template, you can create strong brand messaging and change the verbiage so it works *for* you instead of against you.

Most brokers allow you to change the template verbiage in a website to something more custom to you and your market, and by all means, you should. The language you're given on a template is just placeholder. The person who wrote it doesn't know anything about you or your target market. They wrote it in a very generic way, as a starting point, with the understanding that you are going to take the time to customize it for yourself. Yet a shocking number of advisors don't because they don't want to take the time to do it, they don't think it matters that much, or they don't want to deal with compliance scrutiny.

If you're in that group, you're not alone, but I can't encourage you enough to update your content anyway. I know it takes time, but it's worth it because when someone is referred to you and they go to your website to check you out, they'll see that what you say lines up with what they need, and they'll confirm for themselves that you're the right person to talk to.

WRITING A WEBSITE

Your brand messaging is all the information about your firm—who you are, what you do, how you do it, and what makes you a good choice as an advisor.

At my agency, our approach when working with a new client on their brand messaging is to write it for their website because a website is the one place that tells your whole story. It should have everything on it that someone might want to know about you during the vetting process, all geared toward your specific target market segments.

Sounds simple, huh? Like tying a shoe or something.

In all seriousness, I know writing an entire website sounds super intimidating and like it's going to take forever, but it's really not that bad. And the best part is, when you're done, you're done for good. You won't ever have to start at square one again. And remember, you're not just writing your website. You're writing your brand messaging *for* your website, and once you're done, the same messaging is going to roll downhill into everything else— your company brochure, your social media profiles, even your verbal elevator pitch. Your website is the one place that tells the whole story, and everything else tells a condensed version of it.

THE FIVE CONTENT CATEGORIES

One of the hardest parts of writing a website is knowing what to write about, so let's break it down.

All website content for a financial practice is going to fall into five categories. Four are critical and must be on the website in order for it to do its job of attracting and converting prospects, so let's look at those first.

1. Core Message—The brand promise and elevator pitch of the company
2. Who You Are—Information to help them get to know you, your team, and your company
3. What You Do—Information on your services, expertise, and process
4. Calls to Action—How to get in touch with you and take the next step
5. The fifth category is a catch-all that I call "Optional Content" (very creative, I know), and it encompasses everything else

that you want to put on your website that's not critical to the website doing its core job of attracting and converting prospects. This content varies for different advisors and different practices, and we'll explore some common optional content types later in the chapter.

Let's look at each of these categories in more detail.

CORE MESSAGE

Your core message is comprised of a brand promise and your elevator pitch. On a website, it's usually what you see on the home page in the form of a headline, subheadline, and a paragraph or two that give a high-level overview of the firm.

The brand promise is the headline and subheadline part, and it's where you'll concisely articulate who you work with and what the ultimate benefit is of working with you. If you do financial planning, the deliverable you give people is a financial plan, but what's the benefit to your clients of having one? Some options to consider would be:

→   They can retire when and how they want
→   They'll have the financial confidence to pursue their dreams
→   They'll maximize and protect what they've worked so hard for

When you think about the ultimate benefit of working with you, keep your target market segments in mind and ask yourself if it speaks to their core desires. If someone followed all of your advice through the years, would it result in what you wrote? If so, you've got yourself a winning benefit, and now you just have to merge it with who you work with to create your brand promise.

Your brand promise can either be a single headline, or a combination headline and sub-headline. Here's an example of both approaches:

EXAMPLE 1

Helping Physicians Retire When and How They Want since 1992

EXAMPLE 2

Live Your Best Life

Giving young professionals the financial confidence to pursue their dreams

---

Moving on to the elevator pitch, this should be a few paragraphs that explain who you are, what you do, and who you do it for, highlighting any points of differentiation that separate you from other advisors. To get started on writing it, ask yourself these questions and write the answers down completely:

→ If you met a stranger at an event and they asked what you do for a living, what would you say?
- Sample answer: I own a boutique financial planning firm in Minneapolis.
→ If the stranger dug deeper and asked what your specialties and areas of expertise are, what would you say then?
- Sample answer: I work with business owners and successful professionals to help them grow and protect their assets and balance their current financial needs with saving for retirement.

→ If someone interviewed your best clients and asked them what they like or appreciate about working with you, what would they say?

- Sample answer: I treat them like they're family. I listen and take time to explain things. They trust me to look after their best interests, and they know I'm always available when they need me. Also, I've been doing this for eighteen years, so I have a lot of planning knowledge and experience.

→ What do you find rewarding about what you do?

- Sample answer: I just love making a difference for people and leaving them better than I found them. I enjoy explaining things to people and watching them have aha moments and helping them get on the right path to their ideal future.

Now let's pull it all together and see how the brand promise and elevator pitch from our above sample become a core message.

Helping successful people find the right path to their ideal financial future

As a boutique financial planning firm in Minneapolis, we've been helping business owners and successful professionals grow and protect their assets for nearly twenty years. Through an education-centric approach, we work together to help them find the right balance between enjoying life now and protecting the future.

Our clients are like family to us, and they have peace of mind knowing that we're looking after their best interests through every season of life. We pride ourselves on going above and beyond to give them the outstanding service they deserve, and they know they can count on us to be there anytime they need us. If you're looking for a firm to help you get on the right path to your ideal future, we'd love to talk.

WHO YOU ARE

This section of your website should cover you and your background in great detail, as well as the staff members and strategic alliances who round out your team. The most important advice I can give you about this section is not to go light on content. Other than the core message, there is nothing more important than the information about you. No matter whether you're an individual advisor or you have a big firm, people hire people. And when they're on your website, they're there to vet *you*.

YOUR BIO AND BACKGROUND

A lot of advisors make the mistake of having a chronological bio that starts with the past and ends with the here and now. As interesting as your life story may be, it's not the right format when someone is vetting you. Instead, you should start with who you are and what you do right now, then go into the details of what led you there, and then finish it up with some personal details to round you out as a whole person.

When it comes to the personal stuff, some people like to share a lot and others prefer to share as little as possible. Like I always tell my clients, everyone has a different privacy threshold, and there's no right or wrong. But if you're comfortable lifting the veil and letting people get to know you as a person, it's better from a marketing perspective. Some advisors will go so far as to include a separate personal bio along with personal pictures of their family and hobbies, and their clients absolutely eat it up. It humanizes them and gives people something to connect with and relate to. Plus, there's something very open and honest about showing your real life, and it builds trust almost instantly.

If you're a more private person, that's okay, but I would suggest including some details that are going to feel personal without being too personal. For example, you could end your bio with your favorite motivational quote, a list of fun facts like your favorite book or bucket list vacation, or share a little about the charities you support. All of these details are going to work as connection points without revealing very much about you or your family.

The last tip on the bio is to write it in third person if you have a team or a company name to operate under. Writing in the company's voice instead of your own makes it easier to write about your strengths and accomplishments in a way that doesn't come across as bragging. The only exception is on LinkedIn, which we'll cover later in the book. There, your bio is in résumé format—first person in your own voice.

FREEBIE

For help writing an interesting, effective, well-organized bio, download our free "DIY Bio Guide" at TheReferralMagnet.com.

OTHER TEAM MEMBERS

If you have staff or other advisors on your team, they should have bios on your website as well, especially if they're client-facing, permanent team members. If you have a temporary intern or something like that, it's fine to leave them off. Otherwise, you should include information about everyone on the team.

The bios of staff members don't need to be as detailed or extensive as the bios of advisors because people are not there to vet them, but they should cover what their role is on the team and give a personal connection point or two.

STRATEGIC ALLIANCES

It's a good idea to also include information about your strategic alliances. Depending on your practice, this may be comprised of your broker, the CPAs and attorneys you partner with, or any other person or company that your clients may come in contact with as they work with you. It's a good idea to explain who they are on your website, what your relationship is with them, and why you partner with them.

Sometimes the advisors I work with are hesitant to talk about their brokers because they want to be known as an independent firm, not an affiliate of a larger company. Even though I understand the concern, ignoring them altogether is not usually the right approach. In most cases, your clients and prospects are going to be exposed to your broker at some point when they get paperwork or statements from them, so it's best to explain it up front and position them the way you want to. If you don't, you run the risk of confusing them later—or worse, making them feel like you weren't honest.

The reality is that you chose your broker for a reason, right? They have strengths as a company, and you believe in what they offer or you wouldn't be with them, so that's what you should focus on.

One of the best ways to position your strategic alliances is through an org chart where you and your client are together at the top, and then it branches down to everyone else with a little snippet about what each company or person does. It's a visual representation that showcases your alliances at a glance, and it's great to use on your website and company brochure.

COMMUNITY INVOLVEMENT

If you're involved in local community organizations, it's good to share that on your website. It gives people a better understanding of who you are as a person and what you care about, and it can create a connection point where prospects and clients can find something that they have in common with you.

If you're worried that it will come across like you're bragging about your good deeds, don't be. All you need to do is mention that you're a supporter of each organization and then give a few sentences explaining what they do. You're basically sharing why you support them, and in doing so, it subtly makes a positive statement about your values.

OTHER "WHO YOU ARE" CONTENT

If you have any other information that will help people understand the "who" part of your business, feel free to include it. Some advisors have things such as company history, mission and vision statements, core values, fun facts, office photo galleries, and awards and accolades, and all of that content is great to include if you have it. Anything that helps you to lift the veil and give people a peek into your world will be advantageous from a marketing standpoint as long as it's not controversial. If you have a personal passion that might be polarizing, like politics for example, you're better off not including it unless you're okay with turning people off who don't share your same viewpoints.

WHAT YOU DO

The next section of the website is the information about what you do and who you do it for. This is where you're going to talk about the specific services you offer and what you specialize in, and there are a lot of different ways you can organize everything to make it easy for people to digest. Some advisors will divide this section into target market segments, with each market having its own page about the common services you provide to them and what your process is. Others prefer to have a page about who you work with, a page about your services and areas of expertise, and a page about your process. Regardless of which path you choose, those are the subjects you need to cover.

WHO YOU WORK WITH

Think about the target markets you work with now (and the ones you want to work with in the future) and be sure to mention all of them in the "What You Do" section. Referrals will often look there for final confirmation that you do, in fact, work with people like them.

If you have a lot of client types to include, you're better off just listing them and not going into a lot of detail about each one. Pay special attention to the order you put them in, though, because people will subconsciously conclude that the client types you list first are the ones that you work with the most.

If you don't have too many target markets, you can write a little about each one to demonstrate your knowledge about their needs. This is especially important with clients who have unique financial situations that require a high level of expertise. For example:

→ Physicians—late career start and significant debt, but with high earning potential
→ Business owners—balancing personal and business financial needs
→ Athletes—very short careers but with high earning potential
→ Actors—very inconsistent income but with high earning potential

SERVICES AND EXPERTISE

You want to be sure that you have a comprehensive list on your website of every single thing you do for clients because you never know what a referral is vetting you for. Even if it's a service you don't do very often or you don't enjoy doing, you should list it anyway because it might be the foot-in-the-door service that brings you a new client who you can then offer other services to as well.

In terms of deciding how much detail to go into about each service, I'll give you the same advice as the "Who You Work With" section. If you offer a lot of services, it's best to just list them in some sort of categorized way instead of going into a lot of detail about each one. If, on the other hand, you offer only a few services, you can write more about each one, especially if they require specialized knowledge.

People don't read websites; they skim them. So you want to make it as easy as possible for them to skim and find the things they're looking for. Here are a few tips to consider:

→ Instead of one long list of services, consider organizing them into categories of related services, like "Services for Your Business" and "Services for Your Family."
→ If a service goes by more than one name, like Exit Planning and Succession Planning, list both.
→ Pay attention to the order you list your services in, putting the most important ones first.
→ If you want to make your lists more visually interesting, consider adding pictures or icons.

YOUR PROCESS

Another great thing to include in the "What You Do" section of your website is an overview of your process. Explain to people how you work so they know what to expect. When you onboard a new client, how many meetings are there and what do you cover during each one? What role do you and the client each play? How long does everything take, and how often will they hear from you? These are some of the questions you should answer as you explain your process to prospects.

If you don't really have a defined process and you just play it by ear with new clients, now's the time to change that. Every client is different and it's great to cater your approach accordingly, but you should have some general steps you follow every time—that's your process.

As you're explaining it, you don't need to go into a lot of detail about each stage. A graphic showing the steps of your process along with a couple of sentences or bullet points about each one is more than enough.

> **PRO TIP**
>
> Consider naming your process and trademarking it. Even if the steps you follow are common in the industry, when you name your process, it becomes a proprietary component that sets you apart from your competitors.

HOW YOU GET PAID

The last part of the "What You Do" section is an explanation of how you're compensated, and it's optional to include but definitely on the rise. As much as you may wish people didn't care about how you earn your money, they do, so it's becoming more and more common to include something about it on your website and other marketing materials.

There are two different approaches with this, and they both work well for different advisors. The first is to explain how you get paid without getting into specific numbers. If you're fee-based only, you could have a page about how and why you've chosen that route and how it benefits your clients. If you do both fee-based and commission-based work, you could do a split-screen page explaining both methods and when you use each one. This approach answers the question *how* you get paid without getting into *what* you get paid.

The other approach is to include both the how and the what, and if you go this route, it's best if you have different packages that cover different needs. People like options, and that's why when you go to buy something on many websites, you're given three packages to choose from. One option is usually cheap but too basic, one is overkill and too expensive, and then there's one in the middle that fits just right.

That's called three-tier pricing, and it's a commonly used marketing formula that works very well because it helps people to see the value in what they're getting. Most companies that price things that way are trying to drive people to the sweet spot in the middle, but you don't have to structure your packages that way. Just come up with three different packages with different levels of service for different needs and budgets, and people will find the one that fits best. When it comes to the fee part of the package, I recommend listing ranges instead of hard numbers—planning fee of $2,500–$7,500 with 1.1–1.75 percent annual AUM. This approach will help you appeal to more people and it gives you more flexibility when you're eventually sitting across the table from them.

Of course, you can always choose to not include anything about how or what you get paid on your website. Historically, this has been the most common approach because most advisors want to get the prospect in the door first, but more and more are starting to include some type of compensation information. If that trend continues, you may have to start including it or it's going to raise a red flag, but for now, it's still optional.

The best advice I can give you is to do a gut check about which route instinctively feels right for your practice and go for it. If you choose to include it, you'll want to monitor your website analytics over time to see if your instincts were right. Specifically, pay attention to that page's bounce rate. If it has a high bounce rate, that means a lot of people are leaving your site from that page, so it's hurting your conversions and you should either change or remove it.

CALLS TO ACTION

When a referral comes to your website, the hope is that they will check you out, be impressed, and take the next step. The calls to action on your website are that next step, and you want to give them as many different ways as possible to do it.

I once spoke with an advisor who hated email and thought it was impersonal, so he wanted to put his phone number on his website as the only way to get in touch. I explained to him, "Just like you hate email, other people hate talking on the phone, so do you really want to turn away the prospects who aren't comfortable calling?" Lucky for him, he listened to me.

Let's look at some different calls to actions for your website to help your referrals take the next step.

→ Request a Consultation—This is the most common call to action and the one that gets used the most often by referrals.

They came to your website to vet you, and now that they have, they're ready to meet. It's good to have your phone number, email address, and a form they can fill out so they can reach out however they want to.

→ Schedule a Consultation—This is different from *requesting* a consultation because they're actually booking the appointment to meet with you. There are many services, such as Calendly and Schedulista, where you can plug in your availability and then embed a calendar into your website where they can see your openings and book one.

→ Contact Our Office—Include your office address, phone number, email address, and hours of operation so they know when they can reach you.

→ Connect on Social Media—Include icons with links to all your profiles, and make sure your website developer sets the links to open in a new tab so they don't lose your website when they go to your social media profile.

→ Ask a Question—Sometimes people aren't ready to schedule a meeting because they have a question or two they need answered first. Make it easy by including a form that has fields for their email address and whatever questions they want to ask.

→ Send a Referral—Make it easy for your existing clients and COIs to send you referrals by having a form they can fill out on your website. In addition to their name and their referral's name and contact information, also include a field where they can give you any notes about the person they're referring.

→ Join Our Email List—For people who are not ready to meet with you yet but might want to in the future, it's good to have a call to action where they can give you their info to keep in touch. Giving them a chance to opt into your email list or newsletter distribution is a great approach.

→ Download Our Free Report—Adding a free report, white paper, or e-book to your website is a great way to capture the names and email addresses of people who aren't quite ready to meet with you yet. They input their information, giving you a way to communicate with them in the future, and in return, they get a valuable piece of content from you. Win-win.

PRO TIP

Anytime you have a form on your website, don't go overboard with the fields. Sure, it would be nice to know where they live, how old they are, and what their net worth is the first time they reach out, but if you ask things like that, your form is going to become intimidating and visually overwhelming, and fewer people will fill it out.

OPTIONAL CONTENT

At this point, we've covered the essential content that your website has to have in order for it to work. Your prospects will know about you, your company, your alliances, your experience, your services, and more, and they'll have lots of options to choose from to take the next step with you. If you stopped here, you'd have an effective website that would do its job of impressing the prospects who are vetting you and inspiring them to reach out.

Depending on your practice, though, there may be some additional content to consider that would make the website even stronger. One of the great things about optional content pages is that they give search engines more ways to find you. Some of these content topics, like speaking and educational content, also add credibility to you as an advisor for potential clients.

Here's an overview of some of the more common types of optional content.

SPEAKING AND SEMINARS

Educating others, especially from a stage, adds instant credibility. It shows clients and prospects that you have authority, confidence, and valuable knowledge to share. If you do any professional speaking or host seminars for clients and prospects, that is definitely something you should include on your website.

There are two types of seminars that advisors host:

1. Private seminars: These are educational events where the attendees are all from the same company or community organization, and they have asked the advisor to come do a presentation. For example, we have a client who does quarterly seminars at a local hospital to explain disability insurance options to resident physicians.
2. Public seminars: With a public event, you might book a conference room at a hotel and give a presentation about retirement planning and invite seniors in the community. These self-hosted events can be a great way to meet new prospects and share your expertise with members of the community.

Either way, speaking to groups conveys authority and positions you as an expert in your field. So if you host seminars or do speaking events, consider having a page on your website devoted to the details. You can include:

→ Topics you commonly cover

→ Upcoming events/dates

→ Registration options

You can add a form for someone interested in booking you, a calendar of your upcoming events, or a prospect form for someone who's interested in hearing you speak and wants to know more. As an added bonus, if you have video of yourself speaking, you can include snippets or the entire dialogue with a simple button that says, "To view past seminars, click here."

PRESS AND MEDIA

Being in the media is always impressive (as long as it's "good press," of course). If you've been quoted in articles, featured in a magazine, or won awards, put it on your website! This is a great way to "brag" about yourself because someone else has already done the bragging. Again, you build credibility for yourself when other people have already vetted you as an expert, and this type of credibility is a great way to convert a referral to someone who trusts you enough to become a client.

EDUCATIONAL CONTENT

Prospects visit your website to vet you before they become a client, but do they ever return to your site once they're working with you? You want people using your website regularly for a couple of reasons: not only does it keep you at the top of your clients' minds for financial advice, but it also helps search engines see that people like to visit your site, which in turn can help you rank higher in search results.

Educational content can keep people on your site longer and bring them back to your website later (both are bonuses for SEO, which we'll discuss in a later chapter). Below are some common examples.

Blogs

I endearingly refer to blogs as the junk drawer of a website. Blogs are the place where you can put all the information that doesn't fit anywhere else. For instance, you might want to write about *Overcoming the Financial Impact of COVID-19*. This is a great blog idea because it's important and timely but not necessarily something that fits anywhere else on your site.

Search engines also love blogs. Having a blog and updating it regularly with custom content is one of the best things you can do for SEO. Your blog posts can be video-based, text-based, or both, as long as it's *your* custom content. Using the generic, pre-written blog posts that often come on template websites will not only be unhelpful to you; it will actually hurt your rankings in search engines. If you don't have the time or desire to write your own content, there are plenty of services, freelance writers, and companies that can write posts for you.

Podcasts

If you're more of a conversationalist, podcasts are a great way to share your thoughts with busy commuters or anyone else who would rather listen than read. As of the writing of this book in 2020, podcasts are the "it thing" right now, and more people than ever are getting their information and news from podcasts instead of traditional media and online resources. Recording podcasts is easy and doesn't require a ton of equipment, so if you've thought about starting a podcast, I'd encourage it. If you already have one, put it on your website. Podcasts perform best when they have a theme, like *Retirement in Your Forties*, and themes can help you develop content more quickly.

Newsletters

If you have a company newsletter, your website is a great place for people to read it and subscribe to it. Not everybody who visits your website is ready to schedule a consultation with you yet, so having a secondary call to action, like subscribing to a newsletter, can be a great first step to building a relationship and eventually working together.

E-books

Just like newsletters, e-books are a great way to trade your expertise for a prospect's contact information. Maybe someone on your site is not ready to meet yet, but if they see an opportunity to download a free e-book on an enticing subject, they may be willing to trade their contact information for it. If you're not a writer, that's okay. You can work with a professional writer to help you develop the content, then promote it on your site.

You can set up your e-book so that it's automatically sent to anyone who fills out the form on your website ("For our free e-book, *Nine Income Tax Mistakes Most Business Owners Make*, fill out your name and email here!"), but I recommend sending the e-book manually so you have the opportunity to personalize the email to your prospective client. That way, you've already started a dialogue with them and shown them you take the time to speak with people individually.

Videos

If you have created custom videos about financial topics, or if you subscribe to a service where they provide you with their educational videos, consider hosting a library on your website where prospects can view videos sorted by topic. Video is what marketers call "sticky content" because they keep people on your website longer, which is great for SEO and for conversions.

Calculators

Many advisors have calculators on their websites to answer questions like, "How much longer before I can retire?" and "Am I saving enough to retire by age sixty?" Candidly, they don't get heavily used on most advisors' sites, but they're not going to hurt to include if you'd like to have them available. Sometimes they can be great for you to pull up and use in the middle of a client meeting.

Glossary

The world of finance is increasingly complex, and so is the vocabulary that goes with it. Instead of having your prospects Google "REIT" or "529 Plan," you can have a page on your own website with a list of commonly used financial terms. Some website companies for financial advisors already have a glossary plugged into their templates.

CLIENT DASHBOARD

Client dashboards or portals are a great place to house the information and resources your current clients commonly use when working with you. Your dashboard might contain items like change-of-address forms, policy updates, or documents you usually have to fax or email to your clients.

They are also a great place for people to log into their accounts, see their assets, and check the progress they're making toward their goals. You can also include a place for them to request a meeting with you. If you use Calendly or a similar platform, your clients can view your calendar and schedule a time to meet with you without any back-and-forth emails.

THE WHOLE PACKAGE

Like I mentioned at the beginning of this chapter, there are two separate parts to your website: what it says and how it looks. What you say will only make an impact if people stay on there long enough to read it, and that comes down to it looking good and being well organized. Simply put, you need the whole package.

CHAPTER SUMMARY

→ Your website is the one place that tells your entire story, so when you write your website messaging, you'll actually be writing your brand messaging as well. You can then take elements from it for other things, such as company brochures and social media profiles.

→ There are four critical categories of content that must be on your website: your core message, who you are, what you do, and your calls to action.

- Your "Core Message" content is like the elevator pitch of your brand. It should include your brand promise and the problems you solve for your clients, and it needs to highlight what they can expect from working with you.
- The "Who You Are" section on your website helps clients get a peek into your world and makes them feel more connected to you. This section can include your bio, information about your team, your broker, your community involvement, and even your family and personal life.
- The "What You Do" portion of your website should cover your services, areas of expertise, process, and who you work with.
- Your primary "Call to Action" should be simple, direct, and encourage prospects to take the next step. You can also have a secondary call to action for those who are not ready to meet yet but want to stay in touch.

→ Including additional content on your website like a blog or press releases gives you a chance to build credibility and improve your search engine optimization. Just make sure it doesn't overshadow the important elements.

Now that you know what you want to say and how to say it, let's get into how it should look and function in the next chapter.

CHAPTER 8

WEBSITES

Imagine walking into a doctor's office for the first time and noticing that it smells a little funny, the furniture has a few stains and rips, and everything just looks old and worn out. He could be the most capable doctor in the world, but his office doesn't inspire confidence.

As much as we may not like to admit it, we all make snap judgments about other people's professionalism based on what their environment looks like, and that's never more true than when it comes to your website.

When somebody visits your website, it's often their first encounter with you. Maybe they saw an ad you ran, or maybe they were referred to you, but either way, they don't know anything else about you. They've never met you. They've never been to your office. They don't know how great of an advisor you are or how much you can help them, and as cliché as it sounds, you never get a second chance to make a first impression.

The reality is that the look of your website reflects how on top of your game you are. Do you care enough to keep things modern and current? Do you take your business seriously? How hard are you trying? How detail-oriented are you?

When prospects come to your site, they're there to vet you, and everything they see is either going to encourage them to call you or push them away. They're looking to either disqualify or qualify you, and you want to make it easy for them to give you a gold star.

In the previous chapter, we covered your brand messaging, and you're certainly going to use it here. But now we need to add the rest of the ingredients—everything else that makes a great website and a great first impression.

THE NECESSARY COMPONENTS

Websites are part art and part strategy, and there's not a one-size-fits-all approach that works for everyone. Different websites are right for different advisors, but there are three criteria that all websites have to meet in order to be effective.

CRITERION 1: IT HAS TO BE MODERN.

It seems obvious to say this, but from an aesthetic standpoint, it's important for your website to look modern.

If you ask a layperson what a modern website looks like, they may not be able to articulate it, but they'll know it when they see it. We all go online every day, so when we see something outdated, it stands out in a negative way because it just doesn't look like the rest of the web.

When websites first came out, they looked a lot like Word documents: black text on a white screen in a narrow window resembling a sheet of paper. There was really nothing to them but verbiage and information. The next evolution of websites looked more like magazines with a mix of text and static, flat pictures.

Nowadays, modern websites have evolved to more closely resemble what we see in the real world. Images appear edge to edge on the screen and everything moves fluidly. Modern websites are an intentional mix of content and decor—the information you need paired with the decorative elements that make you *feel* something and add to the overall experience.

Website trends change over time, just like fashion trends, and that's why building a website is not a one-and-done thing. If you want to stay modern and fresh, you'll have to give it a facelift at least every few years so that it keeps pace with the evolving look of the internet.

CRITERION 2: IT HAS TO BE RESPONSIVE.

In this day and age, people access the internet in many different ways. Some people sit in front of a traditional desktop monitor. Some people are on a laptop. Some people use a tablet, and others are on a phone. You want your website to work properly on all these different devices and formats, and that functionality is called mobile responsiveness.

When the mobile web first came out, the best practice was to have two versions of your website: the regular version and the mobile version. Now, the best practice is to have one website that is responsive, meaning it detects whatever size and shape of screen you're on and serves you an ideal version of the site for your screen. This fluid approach is necessary now because of the enormous number of different screen sizes on the market today. Whether someone is looking at your site from a small phone, or a big-screen TV, or anything in between, a responsive site is going to look great and be easy to use.

Speaking of easy to use, that brings me to the last criterion of an effective website.

CRITERION 3: IT HAS TO BE WELL ORGANIZED.

This one is often overlooked. People tend to focus on making sure a website looks great and has great content. It's true that those things are absolutely necessary, but it's a three-legged stool, and the third leg is organization.

When a referral comes to your site, they have to be able to find what they're looking for quickly and easily or they're going to leave. They're not going to click through every page to see what's there; they're going to click around on the things they care about. So whatever that is, it has to be easy for them to find. Some people just want to know who you are. Others want to know what services you provide. And still others want to learn about your philosophy and approach in the business. It's good to have a little bit of something for all these people, but everything has to be organized so that it's easy to find.

Organization also solves the so-called problem of too much content. Advisors will often say to me, "I know it's bad to have too much content," or, "I don't want a lot of content because I know it's overwhelming," but that's actually not right. You can have all the content you want as long as it's organized well. Done poorly, a super-wordy website can feel like it's going on forever, but a well-organized website never feels like a lot of content, no matter how much is actually there.

What you want to do is group things together in a way that makes it easy for people to find what they care about. You have creative freedom with what you name your pages and what order you put everything in, but try to keep your menu as intuitive as possible so you don't confuse people. Ask yourself, "If nobody explained it to me, would I know what's on that page?" If the answer is no, then you need to change the name.

Below is a navigation menu from a well-performing website so you can see how the advisor grouped similar content together.

Who We Are

→ Company History
→ Vision and Values
→ Meet the Team
→ Strategic Alliances
→ Community Involvement

What We Do

→ Our Holistic Process

→ Services for Physicians

→ Services for Businesses

→ Services for Retirees

News and Media

→ Article Library

→ Quarterly Newsletter

Retirement Seminars

→ Upcoming Seminars

→ Seminar Archives

Get in Touch

→ Contact the Office

→ Request a Consultation

→ Send a Referral

That's just one example of a well-organized website navigation structure, but you can see how a referral or prospect completely unfamiliar with the website could still quickly find the information they care about.

GET PROFESSIONAL HELP

Websites are more complex than they appear, and building a great website is a complicated technical process that, when done well, is a perfect blend of strategy and art.

As an advisor, you may be required to use a specific website platform chosen by your broker, or you may be able to do your own thing as long as it meets the necessary archiving requirements and goes through compliance. No matter what your situation is, you want to customize your website to the greatest extent possible. If that means being able to custom-build an amazing website from scratch, that's awesome and it will benefit you greatly to do so. If that's not an option and you have to use a template, don't lose heart because there's still a lot you can do with a template, especially if you have a good web developer.

Working with a professional instead of trying to do your own website is ideal because your website is your most important marketing and branding tool by far, and it affects every single referral and prospect that comes your way. Remember, whether someone is referred to you, you meet them somewhere, or they see an ad you run, their next step is not contacting you—it is checking you out to decide if they're going to contact you, and your website can make or break the deal. Simply put, it's worth the investment of hiring a professional to do it for you correctly.

So all that being said, how much will it cost?

In the financial industry, there are advisors who create financial plans for $1,000 or $10,000, and the same is true for marketers and designers: there's a wide range of prices, so it can be worth it to shop around. Any legitimate marketing or website company is going to be happy to have a consultation with you, discuss what you're looking for, show you examples and case studies of their work, and explain how they might be able to help you and what it would cost.

Beyond the costs, there are other factors to consider as well when you're looking for the right person to help you. For example, I would recommend working with a designer who does a lot of work in the financial sector. They'll know the regulations of the industry as a whole, and they will have a better understanding of what you can and can't do according to your broker's rules. I can't tell you how many times I've had advisors come to me over the years to take over a project they started with a web designer who didn't understand their situation or the platform they had to use. They'll spend thousands building a website on Word-Press, for example, only to find out it's not compatible with their compliance-required hosting platform and cannot be used at all.

So if you want to save yourself a lot of unnecessary grief, look for a company that knows your industry and how to work within it, and then try to give them the reins as much as possible. A good designer is going to collaborate with you on your likes, dislikes, and ideas, and you'll end up with a more effective website if you listen to their guidance and trust their expertise.

PRO TIP

To explain to your website designer what style of website you want, it's best to show examples instead of describing it in words. That's because descriptive words mean different things to different people. New clients will often tell me that they want their website to be "clean" or "simple," but that doesn't tell me anything because what one person calls clean, another calls empty. What one person calls edgy, another person calls messy. There's just no meaning in words like that to designers, so it's better to show than tell.

DESIGN FOR YOUR TARGET MARKET

When it comes to what your website should look like, you have to think beyond your personal design preferences.

Different styles of websites will appeal to different target market segments, so it's important that you create your website to appeal to the people you're targeting, not to yourself. If you're a young, tech-savvy millennial, you probably like websites that are highly creative and edgy, but if you build a website like that and you serve older retirees, you're going to frustrate them and turn them off. Likewise, if you're a baby boomer with a very traditional website but you're targeting Gen X families, there's going to be a disconnect there as well.

Without professional guidance, most people (not just advisors) end up building a website *they* like without thinking too deeply about what's going to appeal to their target market. And if you're not a member of your own target market, that can be a big mistake.

Here are some common target markets and my design strategy for them.

RETIREES OR PRE-RETIREES

For this market, you want everything to appear on your website where they're most expecting it. That means navigation across the top, instead of down the side or at the bottom.

Older populations can get visually overwhelmed, so you don't want too much movement or flashy videos playing in the background. You would do better to have a beautiful picture of something serene, calming, and peaceful—something that's not too "in your face."

For the same reason, you don't want to have big chunks of copy with a dark background and light text, which is harder for older eyes to read.

SUCCESSFUL PEOPLE IN THE MIDDLE OF THEIR CAREERS

They don't have time to dig for things. You have to get to the point quickly on sites designed to appeal to this market. You might want to give them two immediate choices when they land on your home page: "Services for business owners" and "Services for families." They choose a path and everything from that point forward is specific to what they chose. With this market, you still want to supplement everything with pictures and graphics to make the site visually appealing, but you don't want to overdo the decorative aspect of it. Get to the point because your audience is busy. Make it easy for them to skim the content by using things such as section headlines, borders, and icons.

TECH-SAVVY MILLENNIALS (AND YOUNGER GEN XERS)

With this target market, you have a lot of freedom with your design. This is a very creative, artistic market segment and they will appreciate a lot of personal expression. They're going to enjoy some of the bells and whistles that might annoy older or busier populations.

If they land on your site and see a video playing, they're likely to watch and engage with it. In fact, they'd rather see video content than read text.

They like to be surprised and delighted, so you wouldn't want to put the navigation across the top because that's expected and boring. Maybe, instead, the navigation is a grid of photos they hover over and click on.

They also like a lot of interactivity, so try to get them involved in the website experience. Offer them quizzes, provide an option to play music while they're exploring the site, or give them calculators to figure out things such as "What age can I retire?"

Finally, this target market wants a site where it's easy for them to reach out and get in touch with you online. That's where they are. They don't want to see just a phone number and email address; they want a contact form to fill out or the ability to schedule something directly on your calendar.

Once you've incorporated the main strategies for your target market, everything beyond that can be built according to what *you* like. If you like pictures of people, great. If you prefer pictures of scenery, that's fine, too. If you like serif fonts, use them. If not, don't. Those kinds of things aren't going to affect how the site performs, so avoid the trap of spending too much time worrying about them.

GETTING FRIENDLY WITH GOOGLE

In order for your website to do its core job of attracting and converting referrals and prospects, it has to be search engine friendly.

To make your site is search engine friendly, here are some basic best practices:

→ Make sure every page of your website has a custom title tag. This is a piece of code that tells search engines and people what that page is about and uses some compelling keyword phrases. If it's your "Meet Our Team" page, for example, the title tag might be, "ABC Financial Group in Anytown, USA | Meet Our Experienced Team." This text doesn't show up on the website itself, but it does show up in the search engine results. For example, check out this screenshot from a search I did today looking for a company to send a wine gift basket to a client. The title tag is the large blue text you see below.

www.wine.com › list › gifts ▾

Wine Gifts - Best Gifts & Ideas for Wine Lovers | Wine.com

Find the best selection of **gifts** for **wine** lovers - from **wine** baskets to champagne **gift** sets.
Shop now to get free shipping with StewardShip or FedEx pickup.
1 – 4 Bottles · Gifts by Occasion · Gift Baskets · Wine & Food Gifts

www.harryanddavid.com › wine ▾

Wine Gifts: Wine Gift Ideas for Wine Lovers | Harry & David

Shop Harry & David for **wine gifts** for any occasion. Our selection of the best **wine gifts**
includes delicious **wine** and cheese pairings, **wine** sets, and more.
Gifts with Wine · Wine Gifts · Wine Best Sellers · Wine & Cheese Gift Baskets

www.wineenthusiast.com › wine-gifts ▾

Best Wine Gifts of 2020 – Wine Enthusiast

Your hunt for the perfect **wine gift** stops here! **Wine Enthusiast** has a large catalog of
accessories, glassware, and decor that any **wine** drinker will adore.
Personalized Gifts · Gifts for Her · Wine Gadgets · Gifts For the Whiskey Lover

www.winecountrygiftbaskets.com › gift baskets ▾

Wine Gift Baskets - Wine Country Gift Baskets

Every **wine** basket is curated with complementary food selected to bring out and enhance the
nuances of these fine **wines**.
Red Wine Gifts · White Wine Gift · Ultimate California Wine... · Sauvignon Blanc

→ Every time you have a photo on the website, include an ALT-image tag to tell the search engines what that picture is. For example, the image tag might say, "Retired couple hugging on the beach." The search engine wants to know what those photos are because it helps them to have context about what's on the page.

→ Anywhere you have your address and contact information listed on your site, you can put in a bit of code called a schema, which confirms for the search engines exactly where you're located, what your address is, what your phone number is, and so on. Identifying these pieces leaves nothing to guesswork. That way, if someone searches for you using a geographic parameter like your city, it will help you be more visible.

→ Avoid putting important verbiage inside of images because search engines can't read it. I had an advisor one time hire me to do an audit of her website to figure why it wasn't showing up on Google, and it was because her whole site was made up of images from a PowerPoint deck she created. She didn't know how to design content on a website, so instead, she designed each page in PowerPoint, took screenshots of the slides, and used that for the content on her web pages. It was a clever idea, I'll give her that, but not a good one because search engines basically saw a blank website.

→ Finally, the most important thing you can do to help your website be search engine friendly is have good custom content. Using canned content from your broker that other advisors are also using will hurt your rankings because of "duplicate content" penalties. It also hurts your conversions because canned content, by definition, wasn't written for you or with your target market segments in mind, so it's not going to produce the same results as the custom-written messaging we discussed in the previous chapter.

Those are some basic things that any professional web development or marketing company can help you with, and they'll make a difference in your search engine rankings.

THE ADA AND WEBSITES

Another benefit to making your website search engine friendly is that it also helps it to be more ADA compliant. The Americans with Disabilities Act is a civil rights law that prevents discrimination based on disabilities. If you have an office, the ADA is what mandates that your building has to have wheelchair ramps and elevators so that people with physical handicaps can still enter. In the same way, the ADA wants to make sure that people who are blind, deaf, or disabled in some way can still use your website and understand what's on it.

As of the writing of this book, any company with at least fifteen employees is required to make their website ADA compliant, but it will likely become the law for all companies, regardless of size, at some point. Even if you don't have to make your site ADA compliant, though, it's still a best practice so that prospects can successfully go through the vetting process no matter what physical limitations they may have.

The good news is that the process you go through to help search engines understand your website is also going to help a screen reader and other disability tools understand your website, so you're killing two birds with one stone. For example, the ALT-image tag "Retired couple hugging on the beach" helps Google to understand what's on the page, and the same tag is used by a screen reader to explain the page to a blind person.

One final note about making your website search engine friendly and ADA compliant is that it evolves over time, so it's not something that you can just do once and be done with it. It's best to have your website evaluated every year to make sure that nothing has changed that's working against you.

I recommend having your website or marketing company do this for you and provide detailed reports on what, if anything, needs to be updated. There are some online services that will evaluate your website for free and give you a report about what needs to be changed, but those free reports are often misleading and intentionally confusing because they're trying to scam you into buying services that you don't need. Unfortunately, when you're dealing with complex things like metadata and programming code, there are dishonest people who take advantage of the fact that most people don't understand it very well. So just be careful who you work with.

UNDERSTANDING BRANDED AND UNBRANDED SEARCH

I talk to advisors all the time who want to know how to get their website to rank higher on Google, and the first thing I ask them is, "Rank higher for what?" Normally, they don't know how to answer that question; they just want to rank higher in general. But that's not how search engines work. You have to optimize your website to rank for specific keywords and phrases, and the strategy is different depending on what you're going after.

All searches fall into one of two categories—branded or unbranded—and it's important to understand the difference so you can decide on the right strategy for you. A branded search is when somebody is looking for you or your company specifically, and it's by far the most common type of search for financial advisors.

An unbranded search, on the other hand, occurs when someone

Googles something like "retirement planner in Dallas" or "CFP near me." That person doesn't have a specific advisor in mind—they're looking for a stranger—and it takes an aggressive SEO strategy to rank on page one for a phrase like that. It's totally doable, but it's a question of whether it makes sense to go after it because it's going to take some serious effort.

As a general rule, when people have money and they're looking for someone to help them manage it and protect it, they're a lot more likely to talk to someone they know or ask for a referral rather than Googling for a stranger. It's not that it never happens; it's just that it's not super common, especially among people who are affluent or even moderately well-off because of what's at stake. If your target market falls into that category, optimizing your website for branded searches is your best bet.

Doing an unbranded search for a stranger is more typical among people who have less on the line, so you need to ask yourself if that's who you're trying to reach. If you work only with high-net-worth clients, then optimizing your website for unbranded searches doesn't make a lot of sense, especially when you consider that it's going to take a large budget over a long period to do it properly.

If, on the other hand, you're happy to work with someone who's just starting out and doesn't have a lot at stake, unbranded search engine optimization could be a good choice.

Since this book is about increasing referrals, not going after strangers, I'm not going to get into the nitty-gritty of unbranded search engine optimization here, but I will give you three quick tips that will help you tremendously:

→ Tip 1: Follow all the advice for search engine friendliness in this chapter.

→ Tip 2: Focus on continuously adding content about whatever subject you want to rank for. If you want to rank for "financial planning for physicians," then you need to have a lot of content about financial planning for physicians on your website, and you need to keep adding to it. A blog is a great way to do this.

→ Tip 3: Get quality links back to your site through off-site directory optimization. List your business in every online web directory you can, including Google, Bing, Yelp, CitySearch, Yahoo!, Yellow Pages, and so on, and fill out every profile to the max.

FREEBIE

For a list of critical web directories, you can download our free "Directory Optimization Guide" at TheReferralMagnet.com.

Regardless of what's right for you—a branded or unbranded search strategy—it's good to know what you're trying to accomplish so you can be on the same page with your web developer or marketing company.

CHAPTER SUMMARY

→ Your website needs to be modern, responsive to any screen size, and easy to navigate.

→ Website design is complex, so it's best to hire a professional with experience in the financial sector.

→ Your website is not for you—it's for your prospects and clients. So make sure it's designed with your target market in mind.

→ Ensure your site is *search engine friendly*, which means it is built to best practice standards so that people can find you quickly and easily when they're searching for you or the services you offer.

→ *Search engine optimization* (SEO) refers to ongoing marketing strategies that help your website rank higher for specific search queries.

→ A *branded search* refers to when someone searches specifically for you or your firm. *Unbranded searches* include generic queries—"financial advisor in Akron, OH," for example. In a referral-centric business where clients recommend you by name, it is usually best for advisors to focus their SEO efforts on branded search.

We've covered everything you need to do to have a great website filled with compelling content that people can find quickly and easily, but that's only one part of your web presence. Referrals will often look to another source when they're going through the vetting process: your social media profiles.

CHAPTER 9

SOCIAL MEDIA

My client Jaime has a social media strategy that works wonders to generate referrals. Every day, she spends five minutes commenting on her clients' posts on Facebook. If they post a picture of their recent trip to Italy, she'll comment on how beautiful the coast is. If they post a picture of their son's soccer tournament, she'll congratulate him on the victory.

That's it.

It has nothing to do with her business—not directly anyway; she's just being social and showing that she cares about her clients' lives.

It seems super simple, but Jaime's approach is extremely powerful. When you comment on someone's post, you build social capital with them, just like you would if you sent a card, called them, or even took them to lunch.

Jaime does those things, too, but they take a lot longer, so she can't do them as often. People post about their lives on social media because they want people to see it. They want someone to care enough to say, "Your vacation looks so fun!" or, "Your daughter is so talented!" Compared to taking a client to lunch or writing a card, which can take anywhere from five minutes to several hours for one person, Jaime can connect with ten or fifteen people every day and build social capital with each of them.

Every week, she reaches seventy-five to a hundred people with a total time investment of about half an hour, and the results are tremendous. Her strategy keeps her top of mind with her clients, strengthens their relationships, increases trust and loyalty, and the result is more referrals from them over time.

YES, SOCIAL MEDIA *DOES* WORK

There's probably nothing in modern marketing more mystifying and misunderstood than social media. Our society has been fundamentally changed in every way by the social media revolution, and whether that excites you or intimidates you, social media is sticking around. If you want your business to be as lasting as the social media movement, you might as well embrace it.

I talk to advisors all the time who either don't do social media at all and don't want to, or they do it but don't feel like it works for them. If that's you, I totally get it, but if you'll give me a chance to change your mind, I promise that by the end of this chapter, you're going to look at social media differently. I'm going to teach you everything you need to know to use social media successfully to generate referrals and grow your practice.

First, let's take a look at some common misconceptions and reasons business owners resist using social media.

"IT'S NOT A VALUABLE USE OF MY TIME."

It doesn't take a lot of time to implement the social media strategies I'm going to lay out for you. Jaime's strategy takes five minutes a day, and there are plenty of other simple ways to use social media effectively that don't require huge time investments. All marketing takes some time and energy, of course, but social media is a really effective and simple tool when you use it correctly. Once you start using the right strategies (instead of posting random financial articles, hoping that something will go viral), I can assure you that it's time well spent.

"MY CLIENTS DON'T USE SOCIAL MEDIA."

Are you sure about that? Take a quick poll and find out how many of your family members and friends are on some type of social media. Recent studies have shown that every generation uses social media in some form or another. In fact, baby boomers and Gen Xers are among the heaviest users of social media platforms like Facebook and LinkedIn.

If you think your clients are too focused on their businesses or that high-net-worth individuals are beyond the world of likes and heart emojis, think again. Research has shown time and time again that a majority of high-net-worth individuals are on some form of social media, and most of them use it daily. New studies are done every year about this, so I'm not going to include specific percentages, but Google it yourself and you'll see what I mean.

Almost without exception, no matter who you work with, your clients are active on social media somewhere.

"I'VE DONE IT, BUT IT DIDN'T WORK FOR ME."

If this is the case, let's start with making sure you understand how social media is actually supposed to be working for you. Consider this:

→ If you ran a TV ad promoting your retirement planning services, the goal would be for people to see it and reach out to you.

→ If you ran a newspaper ad promoting your retirement planning services, the goal would be for people to see it and reach out to you.

→ If you did a post on Facebook about your retirement planning services, the goal would *not* be for people to see it and reach out to you.

The number one misconception about using Facebook for your business is that your organic posts and interactions will directly connect you with *new clients*. That would be nice, but that's more in the realm of Facebook ads, which we'll cover later. Your organic posts (something you simply write and post for free on your personal or business page) will appear in the feeds of only people you're already connected to, not to new prospects. They serve an important purpose, but they're not going to result in strangers seeing them and contacting you.

You're probably thinking, "If attracting new prospects through my organic posts isn't the point of doing social media, then what is?"

Let's take a look at three great social media strategies you can use to grow your practice.

SOCIAL GROWTH STRATEGY #1: STRENGTHENING RELATIONSHIPS

This may seem completely obvious to say, but social media is designed to be *social*. For the most part, people are there to connect with their friends and family and to share what's going on in their lives, not to find companies to do business with. Embracing social media as a place to be social with people, not sell to them, is like swimming with the current instead of against it. Two important things happen when you approach it this way:

→ You get to be more present in your clients' lives. Instead of thinking about you once or twice a year when they have a financial need, your clients think about you every time you post something or comment on one of their posts. In marketing, we call this time with the brand, and it's a very powerful thing. When you're top of mind with your clients, you get increased business *with* them as well as increased referrals *from* them.

→ You deepen friendships with clients who are already friends, and you create friendships with clients who are currently "just" clients. This makes your clients know, like, and trust you more, and that results in more referrals. Think about a friend of yours who owns a business. Don't you want to refer them to others? People love connecting people to each other; it's human nature, and the desire to do so increases when it's a personal friend they're referring.

It's important to note that strengthening relationships through social media is primarily done through your personal profiles, not your business pages, and the distinction is important. Your business pages have other purposes, which we'll discuss in a moment, but relationship building with other people online should come from your personal profile.

It's also worth noting that generating referrals by strengthening relationships can make the results hard to pinpoint. Think about Jaime for a minute. She spends a few minutes every day connecting with her clients on social media. When one of them sends her a referral, they say, "Jaime, my cousin is looking for a financial advisor, and since you always comment on the family pictures I post, I gave him your information."

I'm kidding, of course. They don't say that because it's a subconscious process, but that doesn't mean that her social media comments didn't play a significant role in the referral by keeping her top of mind and strengthening the relationship.

Even though it's not a conscious process, you can still document how social media strengthens relationships and grows your business by tracking who you're interacting with. When Jaime is done with her five minutes of social media commenting, she sends her assistant a list of who she commented on that day, which is then plugged into a tracking spreadsheet where she documents all of her relationship marketing activities. When Jaime gets a referral from someone, she's able to reference her spreadsheet to see what kind of interactions she's had with that person recently to look for trends.

In 2019 and 2020, more than 80 percent of Jaime's referrals came from people she interacted with at least twice on social media in the previous six months. Knowing that helps her determine the ROI on the time she spends doing social media commenting.

SOCIAL GROWTH STRATEGY #2: INCREASING CONVERSIONS

As we've talked about throughout this book, when someone is considering hiring you, they will almost always go through a vetting process first. Most people will go to multiple sources when they're vetting you, usually your website and a social media channel or two, so it's important to look at your business page profiles and posts through that lens. Your social media channels can grow your business by giving you another chance to say, "This is who I am. This is what I stand for. This is how I'm different."

You can think of your profiles like mini websites. Because of the character limits and format, they're not the right place to try to tell your whole story—that's the job of your website—but they are the right place to reinforce the message. Like we talked about in the brand messaging chapter, your core message is your core message no matter where it is, so if your social media profiles are in alignment with your website, that consistency is going to work in your favor for converting prospects and growing your business.

It's important to remember that some platforms are more profile-centric (e.g., LinkedIn, where you have to practically dig to find someone's posts), whereas others, like Facebook, are more post-centric (and it takes a few clicks to find a bio or description). Either way, what you write in your descriptions and what you post are both important because future clients may look at either one or both to determine if you're someone they want to know better and work with.

Your posts are an opportunity to show them that you have your finger on the pulse of what they care about. In my agency, we refer to this as pulse content, and it's pretty simple to do if you're looking at things through your target market's eyes. For example, if you work with business owners, you should post things that business owners would find interesting, such as an article about how to hire your first virtual assistant or a motivational quote about work-life balance. If you work with pre-retirees, you could post an article about the trendiest places to retire or a link to a retirement readiness quiz. We'll cover some specific guidelines for posts in the next section.

SOCIAL GROWTH STRATEGY #3: REACHING THOSE PERFECT STRANGERS

The third way social media can grow your business is to help you reach your specified target market, even without direct referrals. I said earlier that organic social media posts don't go to prospects that you're not connected to, but you can use *paid* social media ads to reach them. And there has never been a more targeted way to reach a specific audience.

When you run TV ads, you choose what shows to run them during to get your message to the right audience. The networks use surveys and other tools to develop a demographic profile of the type of people who are likely to be watching each show, but at the end of the day, you don't have a lot of control over who actually sees your ads. That's how most traditional marketing works, and it's one of the biggest advantages of social media marketing.

On social media networks, you can very narrowly define the exact target market you want to see a post, and after it runs, you know exactly how many people saw it and how many people liked, commented, or shared it. For example, you could target a post about paying for college to parents of teenagers within five miles of your business who have a household income of $100,000 or more. You could target a post about succession planning to business owners in your zip code who are over the age of fifty-five with a net worth of $500,000 or more. You could run an ad about charitable planning and target it to affluent married couples who have donated to a charity in the last six months.

The possibilities are endless, and it makes it a very powerful marketing approach, especially compared to traditional marketing where your targeting capabilities are much more limited.

SOCIAL MEDIA POSTS: DOS, DON'TS, AND I WOULDN'T IF I WERE YOU

Here are some handy-dandy tips and tricks to keep in mind when composing those social media posts.

1. USE YOUR COMPANY PAGE

Write all of your "pulse posts" on your company business pages, not your personal profiles. Your personal profiles should be primarily focused on your personal life, not information aimed at a specific target market. The only exception is LinkedIn, where you want to post on your personal profile, not the company page. I'll explain why in the LinkedIn section of this chapter.

2. DIVERSIFY YOUR CONTENT

Make sure that no more than one out of every five posts (for your business page) is related to anything financial. Even on a business profile, it's important not to just post financial content. You do financial services for a living—people know that. But if that's all you talk about, you no longer come across as helpful; you come across as salesy, and that's going to work against you. For the nonfinancial posts, look for things that would be interesting for your target market segments like my earlier examples for business owners and pre-retirees. The point is to show people that you are in touch with what matters to them and that you're interested in the same things they're interested in.

3. AVOID POLITICS

Don't post anything political. In today's atmosphere, people lose friendships, relationships, even jobs over their political affiliation. You don't want to alienate the very people you're relying on to send new clients your way.

If you still feel the need to post about politics (or anything divisive or that may portray you in a negative way, such as posting pictures of yourself going out and partying), you have to make a choice: do you want to connect with your clients and stop posting things that might alienate them, or is it more important for you to be able to post these things and *not* connect with your clients, keeping that part of your life private for your friends and family?

4. POST REGULARLY

Post one to three times a week on all your channels. The time and day that you post no longer matters like it used to, so just pick what works for you. Don't post more than once a day because it won't benefit you and you'll end up wasting time. You don't want to "go dark" either because people will still be able to find your profiles and it could look like you're not on top of your game, or worse, that you're not in business at all anymore. You want clients and prospects to only find things that are a good reflection of who you are right now.

5. RESPOND TO COMMENTS

Pay attention to the comments on your posts. If people ask questions, answer them. If they make positive comments, thank them. If they make negative comments, address them privately (as appropriate) and delete them. Just make sure you never leave a comment hanging.

6. BE CONCISE

Don't be too wordy on your posts. If you have something lengthy to say, do a blog post instead. Social media is supposed to be brief.

7. AVOID GRAMMATICAL ERRORS

Use proper capitalization and punctuation, and spell-check what you post so that you don't look sloppy, unprofessional, or uneducated. The other day, I saw a financial advisor (who shall remain nameless) introduce an article like this:

"good article for millennials- i.m.o.."

I'm no English teacher, but I can count four glaring errors right there, and that doesn't portray the intelligence and capability I want to see in a financial advisor.

8. WRITE PROFILES CAREFULLY

Similar to number 7, all the text in your profiles should be well written, too. This advice isn't specifically about what you post, but how you come across as a whole on your profiles. Fill out every field that's available to you when you set up your profile, following rules from compliance, of course. This information won't change often, so take the time to do it right. You can use variations of your brand messaging from chapter 7 to do this, changing the verbiage from your website a little bit so it doesn't come across as duplicate content (which can penalize you in search engine rankings).

9. USE PHOTOS AND VIDEO

Use pictures and videos to help your posts stand out. Usually when you share an article, a picture will automatically post with it, but if not, add your own. Posts with images or videos get a lot more engagement than plain text posts. Similarly, use good cover and profile photos, and use them consistently. Everything should reflect the branding on your website, so take that look and carry it through to your social media profiles. If you're in New York and you use a picture of the Brooklyn Bridge on your home page, use that picture as the cover photos on all of your social media profiles as well. Make sure you have a quality version of your logo or headshot and that it fits appropriately in the profile space, whether it's a square or circular format.

10. COMMENT ON CLIENTS' POSTS

Comment, don't just like. When your clients receive likes on their posts, they're probably not going to click to see who liked it, especially if they receive a lot of likes. You won't get the same benefit as you would from commenting because you engaged at a much lower level, and your client/friend probably won't even know you engaged with it. However, most people have their settings set to notify them when they receive a comment, so they see your name appear when you comment. This is also more personal, even if all you have to say is, "Great job. That's awesome!" And because personal touch and thought are key, it's best to avoid the option on LinkedIn to choose a prewritten comment or message. Your client will notice that every comment on his or her "new job" update says the same "Congratulations on the new job!" phrase. You'll stand out if you write something more personal and original.

11. BE CAREFUL WHEN DELEGATING

Be careful who you delegate your social media posting to. Just because your assistant is young and uses social media with her friends doesn't mean she's going to do a good job with your posts. Personal and business social media are two completely different things, so make sure whoever you delegate it to understands the rules you have to abide by and knows what you're trying to accomplish.

As you can see, social media *can* help you grow your business. Now that we've covered how it does that and what you should be posting, let's take a deep dive into the most common social networks for financial advisors. First up, LinkedIn.

LINKEDIN: CONNECTED WITH PURPOSE

Just like Facebook, Twitter, Snapchat, and Instagram, LinkedIn is designed for people to engage with one another. But unlike those other platforms, LinkedIn is focused on business, combining the social aspect with career profiles. It's truly business social media.

Without exception, every single financial advisor should have a presence on LinkedIn (unless compliance doesn't allow you to, but I don't know of any broker that doesn't allow you to at least have a profile on LinkedIn). It gives you an opportunity to highlight what you do in your career now and what you've done in the past. It's an expanded online profile of who you are in business, which makes it very easy for prospects to vet you and determine whether you're the right fit for their needs.

Having a LinkedIn profile is almost as important as having a website, and because you've already determined what to say about yourself in the chapter on brand messaging, building your LinkedIn profile requires very little additional effort.

LinkedIn can be used passively by maintaining an awesome profile or actively by interacting and engaging with other users. Because it's important to at least maintain a passive presence on LinkedIn, we'll first look at the components of your profile, then we'll discuss some strategies for using it actively if you choose to do so.

ANATOMY OF AN AWESOME PROFILE

Let's look at some best practices for creating your LinkedIn profile.

Headshot

At the top of your LinkedIn profile, you have an option for two images: your headshot and a cover image, which is basically a little snippet of decoration.

The best practice is to use the same professional headshot you're using on your website here. This should be a recent, professional photo, not something taken twenty years (and twenty pounds) ago or something you cropped out of the company Christmas party photo. If you don't have a professional headshot, take the time to go get one. Trust me, a headshot that's old or not professionally taken stands out in a bad way and doesn't make a good first impression.

Your cover photo should align with something you have on your website. If you have a picture of your lobby on the home page of your website, use that same picture on your LinkedIn profile.

You want your brand to look consistent across all channels, which means sending the same message and using the same imagery to the greatest extent possible.

Headline

LinkedIn gives you the opportunity to customize your headline (the short phrase directly beneath your name), but a lot of advisors miss this opportunity. Instead of just writing "financial advisor" here (or worse, leaving it blank), think back to the question we talked about in chapter 7, "What do you do for a living?" If you're a financial advisor in Dallas, Texas, who does retirement planning for business owners, a perfect headline for LinkedIn would be:

Financial Advisor in Dallas, TX, Specializing in Retirement Planning for Business Owners since 2002

This has to be fairly concise because you have only 120 characters for your headline. Think about the most important things people need or want to know about you. Here are a few more examples to get your wheels turning:

→ Founder of ABC Financial, Helping Young Families Get a Strong Financial Start since 2003
→ Experienced CFP® Specializing in Holistic Financial Planning for Physicians and Business Owners
→ Helping Individuals & Families Get on the Path to Financial Freedom for More Than Two Decades

Summary

Your summary is the most important part of your LinkedIn profile. This is where you get to make your case and sell yourself. It's your full elevator pitch—all about you.

A well-rounded LinkedIn summary—like a well-rounded website bio—leads with who you are and what you currently do in business. Then it fills in some of the details of how you got there—your background, education, and so forth. Then you end it with some personal connection points about what you do outside of work. The point here is for people to get an overview of who you are as a person.

Unlike your website bio, which should be in the voice of your company talking about you, your LinkedIn summary is you talking about you, so it needs to be in first person. That makes some people uncomfortable, and occasionally I'll have a client tell me, "I don't want to talk about me; I want to talk about my clients and what I do to help them. The focus should be on them, not me."

I get the point they're trying to make with being client-centric, but referrals are not on your LinkedIn profile to read about other people. They're there to vet you and decide if you're the right advisor for their needs, so you have to focus on telling your own story. An employer wouldn't look at a résumé someone submitted for a job and think, "Gosh, this guy sure talks about himself a lot. I can't believe this whole entire résumé is about him!" In the same way, no one is going to think that when they're on your LinkedIn profile.

One of the biggest mistakes I see advisors make is when their brokers require them to have a disclaimer in their summary, they make the disclaimer their *entire summary*. If you work for a company that makes you put your disclaimer in the summary, that's fine. Count how many characters your disclaimer uses, subtract that from 2,600 (which is how many characters you're given for your summary at the time of this writing), and use whatever's left to tell *your* story before the disclaimer. You may not be able to fit your full bio if you have a long disclaimer, but do the best you can.

Experience

The next section of your profile is your experience section. This starts with where you work now, whether you're a self-employed financial advisor or with a certain broker. Just like your summary was all about you and your background, your experience section is all about your business and your services. Even if you *are* the whole business, that's okay. You should still use the experience section to further elaborate on what you do for people. You can talk about your company mission and values, list your areas of expertise, and share the kinds of clients you work with.

In the experience section, LinkedIn also gives you the option of including some of your past jobs. The best practice is to include this if your past work correlates with what you do now: if it's in a related field, or if it makes you more experienced at what you do now. For example, if you used to own a restaurant and now you're a financial advisor working with business owners, it's fine to include the restaurant, but in the summary where you can write more about each job, explain how it ties into what you do now: "I owned this restaurant for seven years. It's where I learned a lot about business finance and led me to where I am now, working with other business owners."

If your past work is unrelated to what you do now, it's up to you whether you include it. I have a few clients who used to play professional sports, and that's such an interesting talking point that it's great to include. If you've bounced around in different sales careers before landing where you are now, that might be better to leave off.

Skills

LinkedIn has a section on skills that a lot of people misuse because they don't understand it.

This is where you have an opportunity to list the skills that you have: succession planning, retirement planning, financial planning, and so on. The biggest mistake I see here—other than not using it at all—is putting in too many skills. The second biggest mistake is including skills that are not relevant to what you currently do for a living.

I have a client who, before I started working with him, had fifty skills listed, which is the maximum. A bunch of them were things like sales, communication, and thought leadership. He even had "employee relations" listed! None of that is relevant to his business as a financial advisor. When I looked at his profile, how would I know what he's actually good at? If he had listed ten skills, I could make a logical conclusion that those ten things were truly skills he has expertise in. Fifty things, however, meant that his skills related to being an advisor were drowning in a sea of other things he thinks he's good at.

Including too many skills or skills that are irrelevant dilutes the skills you do have, but don't skip this section entirely. From time to time, when your connections log into their LinkedIn accounts, it'll prompt them and ask, "Would you like to endorse Joe Smith for [one of your skills]?" It'll choose one of your skills at random (another good reason not to list fifty), and your connections will often endorse you because they want you to reciprocate and endorse *them* for their skills.

So what's more impressive: someone with one or two endorsements each for fifty different skills, or someone with ten to fifteen endorsements for ten narrowly focused financial skills? You see the point.

One last note on skills: you should list them in priority order, with your most important skills at the top of the list.

Education

I get a lot of questions from clients about what to include and not include in the education section, so let me break down the best practices for an advisor.

If you went to college and got a degree, you should include it because it's a great connection point, and because right now, our culture expects smart, successful people to have a college degree. That may change in the near future, though, because we're in a cultural shift and people have started to question whether a degree is worth the money, or if four years of experience is a better way to start their career. At any rate, if you have a bachelor's degree or higher, list it along with any other (G-rated) details about your college life.

Listing fraternities, sororities, athletics, and other organizations you were a part of can help people find things they have in common with you, and listing academic honors can showcase your intellect and hard work. You should obviously leave off anything that your clients might find divisive or controversial, though, especially political organizations in this day and age.

In addition to traditional education, if you have financial certifications or designations from places like The American College of Financial Services, those are great to include in the education section as well. You should add some details about the designation, such as:

Retirement Income Certified Professional®

The American College of Financial Services

The RICP® designation provides comprehensive instruction on building integrated and comprehensive retirement financial plans. A key focus is understanding, choosing, and executing a sustainable retirement income strategy.

If you didn't graduate with a four-year degree and you don't have any financial designations, I would recommend skipping the education section altogether instead of listing things like high school and trade schools. Again, our society is moving away from the necessity of a four-year degree, but right now, there can still be a stigma attached to not having one, especially with older prospects. If the education section is simply not there, it's out of sight, out of mind, but if it is there and it mentions only high school, you're shining a spotlight on a potential disqualifier.

It's fine to list your high school if you also have college degrees or financial designations, especially if you went to a well-known private school or you work in your hometown. It shows that you have roots in the community, and that's another connection point for your prospects to relate to you.

Awards and Achievements

Yes, it's time to brag again! Include all of your awards, accolades, and shining achievements here. This is the place where you're *expected* to share your accomplishments, so don't worry about feeling like you're being conceited. Think of it like a résumé for a prospective employer—would you downplay your accomplishments there because you don't want to seem arrogant? Certainly not, so don't do it on LinkedIn either. People want to work with the best, someone who is great at being an advisor and has been honored for their work, so include your MDRT Top of the Table®, your NAIFA Quality Awards, and any other honors you've earned.

A word of caution, though: You may want to use discretion when it comes to including production awards from your broker. They can send the message that you're a salesperson trying to hit a quota, and you also have to consider how much you want to highlight your broker relationship. If you co-brand with your broker, then you might be fine highlighting your achievements unless they're overtly production-related, like "Top Salesperson of the Year." If you downplay your broker affiliation and promote a DBA as your brand, then you probably don't want to include too many broker-related awards or your cover will be blown.

Contact

When you optimize your LinkedIn profile, there's an opportunity to include your contact information. Fill out every single field you can so people have the maximum number of ways to get ahold of you: website, other profiles, cell number, best time to reach you, best way to get in touch, and so forth.

And this may seem obvious, but remember to update it when something changes. I can't tell you how many LinkedIn profiles I've audited over the years with outdated contact information.

Interests

The interests section of your profile is essentially other companies and organizations that you follow. The best practice here is to follow groups, organizations, and businesses that might be a potential connection point between you and a prospect. Your alma mater, for example, is something you may have in common with someone. Industry organizations are another good one, and if you have a lot of clients within the same organization or company, it's good to add that as well.

I work with an advisor in Nashville who works with a lot of doctors from one specific hospital system, so he has that organization listed as an interest on his profile. It may seem a little strange for a hospital to show up as one of your interests, but think of it as being interested in what they have going on.

BONUS: YOUR COMPANY PROFILE

So far, we've focused on your LinkedIn personal profile, but if you have a DBA, you can also have a separate profile for your company. It's not nearly as robust as a personal profile—it's basically a brief overview of the company, some contact information, and what category your company is in—but it's good to have for a couple of reasons.

First, setting up a company page allows you to upload your logo, which shows up under the experience section once you connect your personal profile to the company page. The only way to get a logo there is by having a company page and linking to it; otherwise, you'll see a placeholder symbol where your logo would go.

Second, having a company profile is another search engine ranking opportunity. When someone has been referred to you and they type in your name or company to check you out online, your LinkedIn company page is just one more thing that can show up in the results, giving them another path to learn about you.

Finally, if you have multiple people working for you—either other advisors or staff members—they can all connect their LinkedIn profiles to your company profile to showcase your team.

The best practice is to have a company profile on LinkedIn, but it is not where most of the power and opportunity is on LinkedIn. Your personal profile is by far the more important asset of the two, and as you'll learn in the next section, it's the profile you'll actively use to find, connect with, and convert prospects.

One final note on your LinkedIn profiles: Once you've built them out and made them awesome, be sure to review them once a year to make sure they stay current. As your business grows and changes over the years, your profiles need to grow and change with it.

GET CONNECTED

Now that your profiles are ready to impress, you're ready to use LinkedIn actively to increase your referrals. The first step is connecting with as many of your clients and connections as possible.

LinkedIn makes it very easy to do this by giving you the ability to sync the contacts from your email account or another database, or upload a spreadsheet of contacts, and they will find all of the people who have profiles on LinkedIn for you. You can either invite all of them to connect with you or just choose certain ones, and you can either write a custom connection request or send LinkedIn's default connection request. As a general rule, if you make the invitation personal, you have a better chance of them accepting it, but that can take a lot of time and may not be realistic depending on how busy you are and how many connections they find for you.

One of the top questions I get on LinkedIn is who to connect with and who to avoid. This goes for when you're evaluating your own contacts to decide who to send connection requests to and who to accept connection requests from that you receive over time. As a general rule, I recommend connecting with everyone in your database and everyone who sends you a request—with a couple of caveats.

First, if they look shady or the profile seems fake, decline it. I got a request the other day from a shirtless guy I have never heard of, so that's an easy no. The more complicated and common situation with advisors is what to do with connection requests from other advisors. Most of my clients are very successful and among the top advisors in the industry, and they get a lot of connection requests from others who look up to them.

If you get a connection request from a competing advisor who is with the same broker, they may just be attempting to expand their own network and virtually rub shoulders with you. If you like to mentor others and you don't mind connecting with them, it's okay to say yes. If not, don't feel bad saying no, especially if you don't know them very well. There is no benefit to you in connecting with them, and sometimes they're attempting to, for nefarious reasons, see your contacts so they can try to poach them.

POSTING AND COMMENTING

Once you've connected with some of your clients and COIs, the next step is posting content to your personal profile a few times a week. Remember to refer to the posting guidelines earlier in this chapter. Even though LinkedIn is business social media and people are there for business networking, they still want to see the social side, the personal side, how well rounded you are. This is a good place to post content about work-life balance or family, motivational quotes, or about the great book you're reading. (In fact, feel free to go post about this book right now!)

When you post something on LinkedIn, not all your connections will see it because their algorithm decides who and how many of your connections to show it to. If you want as many people as possible to see your content, it needs to be engaging for your target market. According to LinkedIn, their mantra for the algorithm is, "People you know, talking about the things you care about." In other words, you have a better shot of your posts going to more people if you actually know your connections and your content is relevant and interesting to them.

If you're posting a few times a week and your content follows the rules in this chapter, you're probably going to get your posts in front of everyone you're connected to monthly. Keeping your name in front of them and having them think of you goes a long way toward increasing your referrals.

Even more important than what you post, though, is your engagement with what other people post. When one of your clients or COIs shares an article, take a few seconds and comment on it. Just think about it—they put something out there that was important to them, hoping it would get the attention of others, so your being interested enough to comment builds up the relational capital you have with them. Over time, this deepens the relationships you have with your connections and turns you into a friend, and that's a powerful place to be. Just like Jaime who I told you about earlier in this chapter, if you spend five or ten minutes a day commenting on the posts from your connections, your referrals will increase over time.

DO YOUR HOMEWORK

Another use for LinkedIn is that it's a powerful tool for learning about people before you meet them. I have a client named Jordan who usually meets with a couple of new prospects every week. Before he meets with them, Jordan's assistant will go on LinkedIn, find their profile, and try to find some talking points for Jordan to use in their meeting like what groups the prospect is a member of or where they went to college.

If he knows his client is a big baseball fan, he can small talk about last night's game. If he sees that they support a charity that he also supports, he can mention it in the meeting.

I know what you're thinking: "Isn't that kind of like stalking, Kelly?" Yes and no. You can definitely take this too far and research them on their personal profiles like Facebook and Twitter, but as long as you keep your research to LinkedIn, you'll be fine. No one is going to get creeped out by you knowing things from their LinkedIn profile because it's expected and normal to look at each other's profiles. After all, it *is* the business social media network.

If you mention the personal vacation photos they posted on their Instagram account, though, you're on your own.

JOINING GROUPS

A lot of advisors don't know this, but LinkedIn has groups you can join that are similar to networking groups in real life. They are a form of virtual networking, which is certainly different than networking in person, but one big advantage is that it doesn't require nearly as much of a time commitment. Look for groups that may be relevant to you: your alma mater's alumni group, a group for small business owners in your town, or groups centered on a subject you have interest or expertise in.

Be part of the conversations taking place in the groups you join—chime in with helpful advice when you can—but an unspoken rule is to never sell in a group. Everybody there knows you're a financial advisor. The last thing you want to do is join your college's alumni group and start asking, "Hey, how many of you have life insurance? Are you saving for retirement?" That wouldn't be received well at an in-person networking event, and it's not going to work here either. Again, they know what you do for a living; if anybody has a financial question, they're going to ask you.

The whole point is simply putting yourself in a place where you can build relationships inside of a community. I'm a part of a financial advisor group on LinkedIn, and I don't push marketing services on anyone, but guess who they reach out to when they have a marketing question? Guess who they refer when their friend needs a website? Me, every time, because I have built up relational capital with them and I'm part of their community. They know me, they trust me, and they think of me when anything about marketing comes up.

As a general rule, I usually recommend starting slow with anything new you do in marketing, but I'm going to give slightly different advice here and tell you to join at least three groups that may have good prospects for you. If you went to college, join your alma mater alumni group. If you work with small business owners, look for local groups of small business owners. If you have a passion for a particular cause, look for groups that support it.

The reason I want you to join at least three groups to start is that some groups just aren't that great, and I don't want you to write off groups altogether because you joined one that ended up being a dud. I've joined some where the members hardly ever communicate, and some where one or two people post constantly and dominate the conversation. Just try a few out so you can find a good one to stay active in.

MINING YOUR CONNECTIONS

I know this book is about getting referrals *without* asking for them, but if you're an advisor who does ask for referrals, then mining your connections on LinkedIn can be helpful. When you're connected to people on LinkedIn, in most cases you can go to their profiles and view their other connections. There is a privacy setting that prevents this, but most people don't turn it on.

Let's say you're connected on LinkedIn to a great client who is a physician at a local hospital. You can go to his profile, look at his connections, and find a specific person you'd like to be introduced to. Then you can reach out to your client and say, "I noticed you're connected on LinkedIn to the new neurosurgery resident, Dr. Roberts. Would you mind introducing us? There are some great new DI policies for surgical residents that I'd love to show him."

Again, I'm not big on asking for referrals because if you do the rest of the tactics in this book, it's unnecessary. But if you're going to, then asking for an introduction by name is a lot better than asking, "Do you know anyone I should talk to?" You have a better shot at getting the introduction, and it sounds a lot less desperate.

The other thing you can do with mining connections on LinkedIn is reach out directly to prospects through LinkedIn's InMail system. Just introduce yourself, let them know who your mutual connection is, and ask them to connect. If they oblige, then you can reach out again and see if they'd be interested in getting a second opinion on their 401(k) or retirement plan. This strategy has nothing to do with referrals, but it's worth mentioning because it works. You may be surprised by how many people out there are open to talking to an advisor; they have simply never been asked.

FRIENDS WITH (INSURANCE) BENEFITS: FACEBOOK

Now that you've got LinkedIn up and running, next up is the number one social media network on the planet: Facebook.

Facebook is still the ten-thousand-pound gorilla of social media. Time and time again, so-called experts have speculated that some new social platform is "the next Facebook," but nothing has ever knocked Facebook off its pedestal as number one.

I realize, of course, that a lot of younger people don't use Facebook as much. But boomers and Gen Xers do, and that's where most of the money in America is, and it's where your clients and COIs are as well.

There are two sides to Facebook, business pages and personal profiles, and they both play very important—and very different—roles in generating and converting referrals. Let's look at the business side first.

YOUR FACEBOOK BUSINESS PAGE

Facebook business pages might be the most misunderstood marketing vehicle on the planet. Oftentimes, advisors think of them as a free way to attract new prospects, so their strategy is to connect with as many people as possible and do organic posts about different financial topics. After a while, they notice that no one is really commenting on or sharing their posts, and they haven't generated any new leads from it, so they write Facebook off as something they tried that didn't work.

That scenario is super common, and it's also totally wrong. The problem is rooted in the fundamental misunderstanding of what the business page is actually for and what the results are supposed to be.

As I alluded to earlier in the chapter, Facebook business pages are conversion tools, not prospecting tools, except when they are used for paid posts. On the unpaid side, when you put posts out there, they go to only a very small fraction of the people you're connected to—somewhere between 3 percent and 10 percent. So if you are connected with one hundred people, every time you post something, it only goes to somewhere between three and ten of them. That's it. Facebook filters the rest out because when people are on Facebook, they're there to connect with their friends and family, not be marketed to, and because they make money by companies paying them to get their posts in front of their desired audience. If you want your posts to get in front of all of your connections, you have to pay to boost them.

So what's the point of posting if no one is going to see it? The point is converting referrals and other prospects who are vetting you. When they go online to do their due diligence and check you out, they will typically look at your website and at least one other source—most commonly LinkedIn or Facebook.

When they look at you on LinkedIn, they look at your profile because that's what's front and center, not your posts. Those require more digging to find, and that's why I went into great detail in this chapter about how to make your LinkedIn profile awesome. Facebook is the opposite; your posts are front and center, not your profile, so that's what they look at to help them decide if they should reach out to you or not.

They're going to scroll through your business page feed and look at the kinds of things you're posting, and that's why you want to make sure they see pulse content that demonstrates to your target market that you have your finger on the pulse of what matters to them.

If your target market is business owners, a good post would be a quote about work-life balance or a *Forbes* article about motivating employees. It's also good to share financial information now and then, but remember, no more than one in every five posts or you're going to come across like you're selling. Never forget that social media is designed to be *social* and people are there to connect with others, not be sold to.

On that note, it's also good to share some personal content on your business page from time to time. No, I'm not talking about sharing what you had for lunch or your views on last night's presidential debate. I'm talking about lifting the veil and letting people get a peek into the personal side of your business. Post about a great conference you just went to. Share a picture of your longtime assistant, wishing her a happy birthday. Those kinds of things humanize you and make you someone who prospects can relate to, and that can help seal the deal.

On the unpaid side of your Facebook business page, the best practice is to post pulse content two to three times a week, understanding that not very many of your connections are going to see it. That's okay because *converting* prospects is the point of the organic posts, not *attracting* them.

PAY TO PLAY

As I mentioned earlier, you can use your Facebook business page for prospecting by doing paid ads. Sometimes people get hung up on this because they think social media is supposed to be free, but that's not true on the business side of things. Just like any other form of media, like television or magazines, social networks make their money through paid advertisements.

With paid Facebook ads, you can pay to reach the people you're already connected to or you can target strangers who meet certain criteria.

Paying to reach the people you're already connected to may seem strange, but it's actually great for generating referrals because it helps keep you top of mind with the people you already know by getting your content in their feeds. You can either pay to boost all of your posts to your connections, or you can just boost certain ones that you want everyone to see, like sharing about an award you won or inviting everyone to an upcoming webinar.

Paying to reach strangers has nothing to do with referrals, but I want to mention it anyway because it can be a great advertising vehicle and it's simple to do. You just create a post, tell Facebook who you're trying to reach and what your budget is, and they will put your posts in front of those people. They show up on their timeline just like the posts from their friends and family, except they are marked as "Sponsored" content.

The targeting possibilities are endless on Facebook because as scary as it is, they know a lot about all of us. You can target people by geographic area, age, occupation, marital status, interests, education, and more. There has never been another marketing vehicle where you can target people with such specificity, and that's why Facebook ads can be so powerful. Plus, you get to set your budget, so the barrier of entry is low. Of course, the more money you pay, the more people you can reach, but if you want to test the waters with a small budget, you certainly can.

LET'S GET PERSONAL

Now that we've covered the role of your business page, let's dive into the personal side of Facebook, which is actually much more powerful for growing your business and getting referrals.

Your personal posts reach far more of your connections than your business posts. Why? Because people are there to connect with their friends and family, so when Facebook decides what to put in people's feeds and what to filter out, they favor personal posts and paid ads, not organic business posts.

That doesn't mean that Facebook sends your personal posts to *everyone* you're connected to, just a lot more than your business posts. When people reach a certain number of friends in their account, Facebook starts to filter the posts they get based on past behavior. If they comment every time a person posts something, Facebook knows they really like that person and they're going to give them more of that person's posts in their feed. If, on the other hand, they skip by most of someone's posts and never like them or comment on them, Facebook realizes that they don't really care about that person's posts and they'll show fewer of them.

So how do you use your personal Facebook profile to get referrals? It's simple. First, you send friend requests to all of your clients and COIs, then you use Jaime's strategy of spending a few minutes every day commenting on what they share.

This strategy works on any social media network, not just Facebook, but remember that Facebook is still the dominant social media platform for Gen X and baby boomers, so you'll get a lot of bang for your buck here.

Be sure that you're commenting, not just liking their posts, because commenting is what breaks through the clutter and makes you top of mind with them. When you take the time to comment on someone's life, you solidify yourself as their friend, and people go out of their way to refer their friends.

If you're comfortable, you can also share your own personal posts from time to time because letting your clients get a peek into your life also strengthens your relationships with them and increases referrals. I'm making this optional, though, because I know not everyone wants to share personal things on social media. If that's you, that's fine, but at least create a profile and comment on other people's posts so that you can reap the referral benefits from being social on social media.

OTHER SOCIAL NETWORKS

LinkedIn and Facebook are the top two social networks used by successful advisors, but when it comes to social media, you want to fish where the fish are. If your clients and ideal prospects are on another social media platform like Twitter, Instagram, YouTube, Pinterest, or Snapchat, you want to be there, too.

You may not be allowed by your broker or compliance department to use other channels for your business, but you can certainly use them on the personal side to grow your relationships with existing clients and generate referrals.

Just remember that no matter what the network is, social media marketing is about strengthening relationships with existing clients, building relationships with new ones, and improving your overall appearance when prospects are vetting you.

CHAPTER SUMMARY

→ You can use social media to become a Referral Magnet in three primary ways:
  - Connect and build trust with current clients
  - Reinforce your brand message and authority to increase conversions
  - Use paid ads to share your content with specific target audiences
→ Social media should be primarily about strengthening relationships and building trust with clients and prospects, not selling.
→ All advisors should have an up-to-date LinkedIn profile. Prospects and clients expect to read about your credentials and experience there, so you can expand on your authority and expertise without sounding like you're bragging.
→ A LinkedIn business page can improve your search engine visibility and provide extra credibility for your brand.
→ Use your personal Facebook profile to connect with clients by commenting on their posts and staying up to date on their lives.
→ Your Facebook business page acts as a secondary platform for prospects to vet you by seeing what kind of content you post.

It's a conversion tool, and your content should demonstrate that you understand what matters to your target market.

→ Paid ads on social media can help you reach a highly targeted audience for a relatively low cost.

Social media is a powerful marketing tool to help you become a Referral Magnet. In the next chapter, we'll learn about two more tools: email marketing and newsletters.

CHAPTER 10

EMAIL MARKETING AND NEWSLETTERS

Remember back in the day, when the internet first came out and everyone just started to have email, you would insert your AOL CD, endure that awful dial-up screeching sound, and wait for that exciting announcement: You've got mail!

No one's excited about getting email anymore, especially not in the business world. As a general rule, everybody wishes they had less of it, not more. Most people get so much junk email and unnecessary notifications that it can be a full-time job to keep up with it.

That's not what we're talking about here.

I'm talking about *good* emails—sending the kind of content people actually *want* to receive, to people who want to receive it *from you*. Don't write off email marketing because you think it's just sending people more spam. Instead, think of it as sending direct, focused information to people who know, like, and trust you.

KEEP IN TOUCH

In this chapter, we're going to focus on email marketing and newsletters—two marketing strategies that are great ways to keep in touch and stay top of mind with your clients, COIs, and prospects who know you but have not converted to clients yet. This isn't about buying lists of strangers and sending them things they don't care about; this is about getting targeted messages in front of people who *already have a connection to you.* The result is stronger relationships, increased business, and more referrals.

Like that old AT&T commercial used to say, you're going to reach out and touch someone.

As marketers, we talk about touches all the time, but what are they and why are they important? Think of touches as any interaction you have with someone in your database, whether it's calling them, sending a birthday card, or emailing an article to read. Your A clients probably get a lot of touches from you anyway because they're your more active accounts and they generate the most revenue. You probably see them and talk to them a few times a year, send them cards, and maybe even hang out with them socially.

But what about everyone else in your database? What about all those clients who just have a small policy with you, or the prospects who filled out a contact form on your website but never converted to clients? How often do they hear from you? If it's not very often, you're missing out on some of the lowest-hanging fruit out there in terms of business growth opportunities. These are people who already know you and have some sort of connection to you, and just because they're not an A client today doesn't mean they don't have the potential to become one tomorrow. And it certainly doesn't mean they don't have the potential to refer you to someone who is an A. That's why you have to have at least a handful of touches throughout the year to stay in front of them.

Email and newsletters are great choices for staying in front of your entire database because neither one of them takes a lot of time or money. The goal is to become a bigger presence in their lives by keeping yourself in front of them, so you're not just the person they call once in a blue moon when they need to change something with one of their policies. When you have a larger presence in their lives and minds, you can educate them on all sorts of financial topics and opportunities, which can turn into increased business from them and more referrals.

This isn't just about getting in front of your connections; it's about keeping yourself in front of them in a compelling, strategic way that helps to build your relationships with them. Staying top of mind and deepening your relationships are two strategies that, when paired together, result in a significant increase in referrals and conversions over time.

Without these strategies, people won't know everything you do; when they need a different type of service, they might not think of you; and you won't necessarily be the first person they think of when they have a friend or family member to refer.

Email marketing and newsletters are tools that you can use to keep in touch with the people you're already connected to—existing clientele, prospects, and centers of influence—so that you remain top of mind and tip of tongue year round.

EMAIL MARKETING

One of the best things about email marketing is the speed of execution. Unlike making individual phone calls to touch base with people, you can sit down in front of your computer for a few minutes and create a compelling touch for hundreds or even thousands of people at once. Email saves time, and because it's free and accessible to anyone, everybody has it.

"But, Kelly, don't people already get too much email?"

Yes, they definitely do—particularly people who are of working age—but hear me out. People are inundated with emails, but it's still a great communication tool *if you use it sparingly*. That's the first key. As long as you're not bombarding people with emails all the time, they will open and read the ones you do send.

The second key is making sure what you're sending is valuable. Put thought into what you send and make sure it's timely, relevant, and interesting. Shifts in the economy, a new insurance law passing, or your state legislature proposing a new bill are good examples of what to share. As a great financial advisor, you're already tapped into what's going on in the world of finance so you can help your clients. So why not occasionally send out a quick email to educate them? Even if it ends up not being of personal interest to them, just knowing they have someone in their corner who's looking after their financial well-being gives them peace of mind and makes them feel well taken care of. And emails are easily shareable, so they can pass the information on to others and expose you to new prospective clients.

Timeliness is important with educational emails because you want your clients to rely on getting news like that from you. When financial buzz goes around, you want them to think, "If it's important enough, my advisor will tell me about it." As you become that kind of resource for them, it strengthens your relationship and increases the likelihood of their sharing your message with others, growing your reach and your business.

Before you begin creating helpful, shareable email content, make sure you know your broker's rules regarding email communications. Some companies require their advisors to get compliance approval on all mass emails, even the ones sent to their own database of clients, and others do not. Some companies allow you to use email distribution platforms, like Constant Contact and Mailchimp, and others require you to send all emails only through your company-monitored email account. Several brokers I work with have a rule that if you send an email to more than twenty-five people at a time, it has to go through compliance, but if you send it in batches of less than twenty-five, it does not. The point is, the rules are different for everyone, so be sure to learn them and follow them so you don't get in trouble.

THE POWER OF YOUR DATABASE

This may sound obvious, but in order to email your clients and connections regularly, you actually have to have their email addresses. You need a centralized database with all the email addresses and other contact information of all your clients, prospects, and COIs so you can send emails to everybody quickly and efficiently.

To take it a step further, it's important to not only have a database but to also have that database segmented in a variety of ways. Most contact management systems, like Salesforce and Redtail, give you the ability to add an unlimited number of tags to each contact, and I highly recommend you make use of this feature. Tag them by what they are to you—current clients, former clients, prospects, or COIs. Tag them by what kind of business they do with you—investments, insurance, planning, and more. Tag them by their net worth, by the stage of life they're in, and by whether they've sent you referrals. The more ways people are tagged, the more targeted—and effective—your marketing can be because you'll be able to download reports of specific groups of people to send specific kinds of information to.

Your database is also a great place to keep track of how prospects are coming to you—the sources of your referrals—so you can see the trends in your practice. When you get referred to somebody, make a note not only of who gave the referral but also what preceded it. "I went golfing with John. A month later, he referred me to Andy." Maybe you get a lot of business when you go golfing. If you're not keeping track of this information, it's difficult to fully understand what's working and what's not. Tracking and keeping good records gives you the ability to see patterns and assess what's working and what's not.

"I usually average twenty referrals a year, but this year I got only eight. What did I do differently? Hmm, I canceled my country club membership and didn't golf as much. Maybe I should get that back."

It may seem daunting when you first start tracking and keeping records like this, but trust me, it becomes second nature and it's extremely powerful.

If you haven't been in business a long time and don't have a huge database yet, it's going to be pretty easy to spend some time going through it and adding tags and notes. If you're like many of my clients who have been in the industry for decades and have thousands of contacts in your database, there's no getting around it. It's going to be a project to add tags and notes, but don't let that discourage you. There are a couple of ways to approach it without getting overwhelmed.

→ Consider hiring an intern or part-time employee to help. They may not know everything to add to every record, but they can at least tag people by what kind of accounts they have, what their net worth is, how old they are, and other data that's easy to look up without your involvement.

→ If you prefer to handle it yourself, I recommend looking at the total of contacts you have and dividing it by 250, the average number of workdays in a calendar year. Committing to tagging twelve records a day for the next year is much easier than sitting down to tag all 3,000 at once.

One of my retainer clients, Sharon, is a very successful advisor with a massive database of clients and COIs that are segmented and tagged about a dozen different ways. They didn't used to be tagged at all, but she hired a part-time college student a few years ago to help her clean her database up and tag everyone, and she would tell you that it's one of the best things she's ever done. Now whenever she reads a great article or comes across something interesting for her clients, all she has to do is forward it to my agency and tell us who to send it to, and we take care of the rest.

"Kelly, can you send this to my 'Advisor' list?" That's the list of all the third-party advisors, like attorneys and CPAs, who she works with. By sending things to them, she builds her value by keeping them in the loop on things that may affect their mutual clients, and she's giving them shareable content that they can send to others. Doing this a few times a year always results in more business and more referrals, and it doesn't cost her anything. It's a very fast, turnkey process that takes her a minute or two to initiate, thanks to her segmented database.

Even if you don't have an agency on retainer to actually send the email, it's still a fast process to do on your own and it's free.

PLAIN OR PRETTY?

I'm often asked if it's best to send plain text emails through a regular email account, or if it's necessary to design emails in a pretty template, like from Constant Contact or Mailchimp. For the strategy that we're talking about in this chapter—emailing your current contacts an article or piece of helpful information—the only advantage of using email systems is that you'll have better tracking. It will confirm that everybody received the email and will tell you how many people opened it, how many people deleted it without reading it, and how many people forwarded it on. You'll have a lot of data, but again, that's the only real benefit.

Research has shown that you'll get the best engagement if the email is short, sweet, and in a format that looks like a personal email from you to them. When it comes in a designed template, an email looks more like a marketing piece instead of just helpful information you're passing along, and that can reduce the number of people who will read it.

Assuming your compliance situation allows you to do both kinds of emails, you'll have to decide which is more important to you: having data about who saw your email and what they did with it or getting your information in front of more people. For most advisors, the latter is more important, but it's really up to you. Either way, here are a few more best practices:

→ Be brief. Use as few words as you can to get the point across effectively.
→ Include links for people to read for more information.
→ Encourage people to let you know if they have any questions about what you sent.
→ Shoot for sending something to everyone in your database three to four times a year. More than that is too much and will start to work against you.

Following these simple tips ensures that you'll get the highest number of views and responses—engagement that keeps you top of mind for your clients and prospects.

PERSONAL NEWSLETTERS

Even though emails and newsletters often get lumped together, including in this book, personal newsletters actually have a completely different purpose and approach than what we just discussed for email marketing.

Emails are all about sharing helpful information and making sure you're the go-to financial resource that your clients and connections rely on. In contrast, personal newsletters are a tool to help you deepen the relationships you have with people by lifting the veil and giving them a peek into your world. Both help you stay top of mind and both increase referrals but for different reasons.

The referrals that stem from informational emails usually come from someone forwarding your email to someone else who they think might benefit from the information. In contrast, personal newsletters increase referrals by helping people get to know you better and feel more connected to you. Just like we talked about with social media in chapter 9, your clients are much more motivated to refer you if they consider you a friend, and personal newsletters can help make that happen.

PERSONAL VERSUS TECHNICAL NEWSLETTERS

If you Google "financial advisor newsletters," most of the results you'll see are for technical newsletters. These are prewritten with financial articles and information, and they're not what I'm talking about in this chapter. If you have a subscription to a newsletter like that, it's okay to keep using it, but I would recommend reading the articles from time to time to make sure they make sense for your clientele. Sometimes technical newsletters will have a section that you can put a personal message in, but the bulk of the content is prewritten financial information created by someone with the masses in mind.

In contrast, personal newsletters may include one section of financial content, but they should primarily contain personal content. No, I'm not talking about sharing your family secrets or what you had for dinner last night. I'm talking about fun, engaging content that's designed to help people know, like, and trust you more. Here are a few ideas you might include:

→ Photos of things that have happened in the office: If you hired a new receptionist, welcome them to the family, include a picture, and give a little getting-to-know-you information about the new voice on the phone or face behind the front desk.

→ Stories from your life and the lives of people in your office: If your junior advisor is getting married or having a baby, show a picture of the new happy family and tell a little bit of their story. Wish happy birthday and happy work anniversaries to your staff members.

→ Charity spotlight: If you and your staff all go to a charity event together or compete in a local 5K, share pictures of it. You can also promote upcoming events and information on the causes you care about.

→ Favorite things: You could share a little about your favorite book or movie, the best new recipe you've tried, or a great vacation spot you discovered.

→ Motivational quotes: Everyone needs a little inspiration, so share a different motivational quote in each newsletter.

Keep most of your newsletter relational because that's what

people want to read. Humans are voyeuristic, in a positive way; we have an appetite to get to know people—especially people we do business with—on a personal level. Newsletters are a great way to feed that hunger, build relationships with people, and help shift the needle from advisor and client to friends.

When you send these kinds of newsletters, the positive feedback you're going to receive will astonish you. People will *eat it up*. They'll talk to you about it, they'll put it on their fridge, they'll even share it with friends and family. It's a great way to market your business that's not overdone anymore. It's a nod to the past but done in a modern way, and people love it.

Here are some additional best practices for creating a great newsletter:

→ A favorite tactic of mine is to have one column that's always the same in every newsletter: a list of everything you do with a message of, "Did you know we offer the following services?" That column makes sure your readers know everything you do, and even though they won't read it every time, they will reference it when financial things are on their mind. It's also powerful because your clients may not know the things you do that are not relevant for them, but those can be referral opportunities. For example, when was the last time you talked to a nonbusiness owner about succession planning? Do they even know you do it? Perhaps not, but what if they have a friend who is looking to sell their business and they're asked if they know anyone who can help? Will they think of you? The column of your services can help with that.

→ Frequency-wise, I recommend sending newsletters either

twice a year or quarterly. Monthly may sound great, but trust me, it's difficult to craft a great newsletter more often than that. If you do it quarterly, you can make it a little shorter; if you do it semiannually or annually, you can make it a little longer. Just remember, it's better to send an awesome newsletter once a year than to send something "meh" four times a year that people will ignore.

→ I like sending newsletters around the holidays, whether that's Thanksgiving, Christmas, or New Year's—all three make sense because you can tailor it to how thankful you are for your clients, or make it a business version of your annual holiday letter, or you can focus on everything you accomplished this year and what you're looking forward to accomplishing next.

→ Keep a document somewhere so you can jot down the things that pop into your mind that would be good for a newsletter. That way, when it comes time to put something together, you already have a list of ideas started. I have a document on my computer desktop all the time called "Parking Lot of Ideas," and something like that will work just fine.

→ Finally, the A+, gold-star way to do newsletters is to print them physically, address the envelopes by hand, and send them in the good old-fashioned mail. I know that's a pain and it increases the costs and time, but it cuts through the clutter and almost *guarantees* it will get read. If you want to do this but don't have the time to hand address, there are plenty of services that will hand-address and mail them for you, or you could hire an intern or a part-time student. If you don't want to send a physical copy to everybody, you can just mail it to your A clients (that's why you have that segmented database after all) and email it to everyone else.

CHAPTER SUMMARY

→ Reaching out and touching clients regularly is important. A touch can be anything from a phone call, to sending a birthday card, or sharing an article of something that might interest them.

→ Don't discount the folks who aren't currently on your A-client list. They can be a potential source of referrals, even if they never turn into an A themselves.

→ People definitely get too much email these days; however, emails that are timely, relevant, interesting, helpful, and shareable can be a powerful way to communicate.

→ Technical newsletters are great as long as you know the content being provided is right for your clients. Personal newsletters are excellent because they satisfy clients' voyeuristic urges to learn more about you, and they can be a great way to connect.

Now that you know how to generate referrals by strengthening your client relationships through emails and newsletters, let's take a look at how to impress your prospects by boosting your credibility in chapter 11.

CHAPTER 11

BOOSTING YOUR CREDIBILITY

My client Ann had been in business for only a few years when she set up her three-step goal:

1. Win NAIFA's Four under Forty award
2. Become the number one agent in the country at her brokerage
3. Make it onto *Barron's* Top 100 list

In 2013, Ann was named one of the top four financial advisors under the age of forty. In 2016, she became the youngest person ever to become number one at her brokerage, and although she's not on *Barron's* yet, at least not as of the writing of this book, that's next in line.

As Ann accomplishes each of her goals, her credibility grows, and her practice grows right along with it.

GET A BOOST

Anytime anyone else says something positive about you and your firm—whether that's in a testimonial, through an award, in a press release, or quoting you as an expert in an article—you want to capture that and share it.

As you know by now, when someone is referred to you, their first step is not to contact you; it's to check you out. Showcasing your accolades builds your credibility and impacts how many referrals you get in the first place, and they help to increase the number of referrals who end up reaching out to you and converting into prospects.

For that reason, you should share your credibility boosters widely and often. Highlight them on your website. Promote them on social media, and use that to drive more traffic to your website. Include them in your next newsletter, or send out an email to share your victories. Each time you do, it reminds your clients that they made a wise decision in hiring you, and it creates shareable content that they can send to the people they refer to you.

If this feels a little too self-centered or like bragging to you, there are two things to keep in mind. First of all, if you have your own DBA, even if you're the only person in it, you'll always share your victories in the company's voice. In other words, it's not *you* bragging about you; it's the company bragging about you. And there's a big difference.

Second, whether you have a DBA or not, when you share your awards and accolades, you can always turn it back to your staff and/or clients. For example, "I just found out that I was named a *D Magazine* 'Best Financial Advisor in Dallas' again this year. I just want to give a heartfelt thank you to my staff and my clients for making it possible. I couldn't do what I do without you!"

Let's look at the most common credibility boosters and how you can use them to your best advantage.

TESTIMONIALS

Testimonials in the financial services industry are heavily regulated. Depending on your licensing and whether you're an investment adviser, you may or may not be allowed to use testimonials at all right now, but there is hope that the rules may be changing in the near future. Fingers crossed!

ASKING FOR TESTIMONIALS

If you *are* able to use testimonials, there's nothing more powerful than somebody else's words saying how great you are.

The most common modern-day testimonials are online reviews, typically on sites like Google, Yelp, Facebook, and LinkedIn. (Yup, a review and a testimonial are the same thing!) For vetting and search engine optimization purposes, reviews on Google will benefit you the most, but once you have several good reviews there, you should focus on other channels so that you're building reviews in multiple places and not keeping all of your eggs in one basket.

If you are close to your clients and you've spent the time building real relationships, then there's nothing wrong with asking them to write a review or testimonial about their experience with you.

However, one *major* word of caution: Do not ever have someone write a review for you who isn't a client. Google and other review services are like Big Brother, and they know a scary amount about all of us and have sophisticated ways to catch fake reviews. If they even think that a review might be fake, the results can be catastrophic to your online presence. I've seen Google and Yelp penalize companies by removing all of their good reviews and leaving all of the bad ones. In other words, you could have twenty great reviews and two bad ones, and then you suddenly just have the two bad ones out there scaring people away.

For that reason, I highly recommend not ever doing fake reviews, and if you want to play it extra safe, don't let your family members and employees review you even if you really are their advisor because they could think it's a fake review and penalize you. I've had that happen to me personally, and trust me, there is no recourse. You can send them records and evidence that you do business with the person and that the review is real, and they still will not care.

Hopefully, I haven't freaked you out too much because even though there are some risks with reviews and testimonials, there are way more rewards and they are absolutely worth getting if you're allowed.

If you want to get testimonials but you're not personally comfortable asking your clients for them, you can either have one of your staff members do it or hire a marketing agency to reach out on your behalf. It can be a lot less awkward for someone else to say, "Hi, I'm Kelly. I help Joe Smith with his marketing, and I'm working on getting some testimonials for him. If I send you a link, would you mind writing him a review on Google?"

THE FEEDBACK PORTAL

Years ago, I came up with a unique way for my clients to generate positive reviews without asking for them and to prevent negative ones. It's a two-part system I call the feedback portal, and here's how it works.

Part One

On your website, in your email footer, and on your social media profiles, have something that says, "I care about providing exceptional service to you. Please take a moment to let me know how I'm doing," and then include a link to a feedback page on your website. Notice that you're not asking them for a testimonial here; you're telling them that you care about your service and you're asking them for honest feedback about it. When they click the link and go to the feedback page on your website, they'll find a form that asks three questions:

1. On a scale from one to five, how good is my service to you? (1 = worst, 5 = best)
2. On a scale from one to five, how comfortable would you be referring me to someone you care about? (1 = not comfortable, 5 = very comfortable)
3. Is there anything else you'd like me to know? (open-ended paragraph field)

Part Two

After they submit the form, they'll be redirected to one of two "thank you" pages depending on their answers to the first two questions. If they chose four or five on both of them, the form will automatically redirect them to a page that says, "Thank you so much for your feedback. I would appreciate it if you'd take a moment to review me on one of these websites as well," and then provide links to your profiles on Google, Yelp, or wherever else you want to get reviews.

If, on the other hand, they chose a one, two, or three for either of the questions, that means there is something they're not happy with, so you don't want to send them to the review sites. Instead, the form will automatically redirect them to a different page that says something like, "Thank you so much for filling out the form. Please know that I take your feedback very seriously. If there's anything you want to discuss, you can call me at this number."

With this feedback portal system, all you have to do is let people know that you care about your service and want to know how you're doing, and the ones who rate you a four or five are the ones you'll get reviews from because you've made it easy for them. The ones who rate you below that will have a place to explain what's wrong in question 3 and get things off their chest—things that might not have been said otherwise. The form gives them a private place to vent. Although nobody likes to read negative feedback, if there's something you or your staff members have done to upset a client, you need to know about it so you can make it right. The feedback portal makes it easy and can help you discover problems that you didn't even know existed.

DEALING WITH BAD REVIEWS

Getting bad reviews is an inevitable part of doing business in the digital age. You can be the best advisor in the world, but you're still going to encounter crazy people from time to time or have misunderstandings that lead to bad online reviews. When it happens, there's almost always more to the story, and I get asked all the time how to go about removing them.

The unfortunate reality is that there is almost zero chance that review sites like Google and Yelp will ever remove a bad review no matter how compelling your argument is. Just like they don't care if a real review is errantly marked as fake, they also don't care if a bad review is accurate or fair. You can plead your case and even submit evidence, but you'll be wasting your time and they're going to leave it there anyway. In my twenty-plus years in marketing, I have seen only one bad review ever removed. It was for a hotel I was working with, and the review was about the hotel being under construction and how they should have warned the guests ahead of time because of all the mess and noise. My client's hotel was not under construction—the hotel across the street was—and we were eventually able to prove it and they removed the review. It's the only time I've ever seen it happen, and even in that case, attorneys had to get involved for it to be taken down.

Even though you can't remove them, there are two very effective things you can do to take the sting out of a bad review: surround it with good ones and respond to it.

The best defense is a good offense, so the first thing you should do is work to get good reviews. If you have two reviews on a particular channel—one 5-star and one 1-star—your average is 2.5 stars. If you have ten reviews on that channel—nine 5-star and one 1-star—your average is 4.6 stars, which is excellent. The best practice is to be proactive at getting good reviews now so that when a bad one hits, it doesn't hurt too much. But even if you already have bad ones out there, there's no better time than right now to work on getting good ones to balance it out.

The other thing you can do with a bad review is respond to it. Most review sites allow you to respond to reviewers, and you should take the opportunity to do so, but be careful with what you say. The tendency is to defend yourself vigorously and point out all the reasons the person is wrong, but that's going to make you look even worse. The right approach is to speak in the affirmative and defend yourself without defending yourself. Here's an example of what I mean based on a real review one of my clients got recently:

"Joe is the worst advisor ever! Do not trust him with your money, especially if you're not white. He makes his living off screwing other people out of their money. Trust me, stay away!"

This is how my client wanted to respond, which would have been the wrong approach: "Are you kidding me!? You lost your own money because you didn't follow the plan I laid out for you. That's your fault, not mine. And I am the furthest thing from a racist. How dare you accuse me of that!"

Here's the correct response: "I'm very sorry to hear that you feel like I screwed you out of your money. As I always tell my clients, there are no guarantees with the stock market and you have to be willing to play the long game. For more than ten years, I've been working with clients of all different ages, races, ethnicities, and religions, and no matter who they are, I do my best to treat them like family and help them make smart decisions with their money. I truly hope that you find an advisor that you like, and if you want to talk further about this or anything else, you can call me anytime at 555-1212."

The first response may feel better to write, but the second makes you the good guy in the situation, and it addresses the fact that you're not a racist or a con artist without sounding defensive. Always keep in mind that when you're responding to a bad review, you're not responding to the person who wrote the review; you're responding to all the people who are going to read it in the future. Make sure you come across as the level-headed good guy, and you'll win every time.

WHEN TESTIMONIALS ARE PROHIBITED

If you are in a situation where you're not allowed to get testimonials, I promised you two alternative strategies you can use to generate similar results:

1. Create a "Featured Clients" page on your website that showcases some of your clients with headshots and bios. The trick, though, is to put quotation marks around the bios. I know it sounds strange, but when you format bios that way, most people will think it's a page of testimonials from happy clients. The reason this works is that you're formatting the page in a way that is common for testimonials, and most people skim testimonials instead of reading them. In other words, they'll click to the page and think, "Wow, that's a lot of happy clients!" and then they move on. But even if they do read them, there's still a benefit because you're telling them about your

clients and the kind of people you work with, and that can help with conversions as well.

2. Another thing you might be able to do in lieu of testimonials is put some case studies on your website. For example, you could tell the story of a doctor with a wife, six kids, and $200,000 in college debt and share the process he went through to become debt-free. A lot of companies allow this as long as you change the names and details and have disclaimers about not guaranteeing similar results, and case studies can be a compelling way for you to share your success stories instead of your clients doing it through testimonials.

If you are able to have testimonials, you obviously should. But if you can't, you can still use these strategies as the next best thing. And even if you can't do *any* of the above ideas, you'll still be able to boost your credibility with one of our other techniques: award marketing, press releases, and articles.

AWARD MARKETING

Local and national awards are another great way of building your credibility and impressing prospects.

On the local side of things, most communities have some kind of annual awards where they recognize the best businesses in a variety of different categories. Familiarize yourself with what kind of awards are available at the local and state level, and make it a point to apply for them because when people are going through the vetting process to decide if they should contact you, seeing that you've won awards can be a big credibility booster.

There are also awards at the national level that are good to go after. Some of the most common ones are:

→ The Million Dollar Round Table (MDRT) Award
→ The NAIFA Quality Award
→ The 5-Star Wealth Manager Award
→ The Women's Choice Award

If you're new to the industry and you're not familiar with these awards, they don't have a limited number of winners. Everyone who applies and meets the criteria earns the award for that year, so they can be a great way to build up your list of awards and accolades.

There are countless niche awards out there as well—for minority-owned businesses, female-owned businesses, veteran-owned businesses, and so on. It's worth going after every single one you qualify for every single year because they really do make a difference with your referral conversions. Most advisors I talk to like the idea of getting awards, but the challenge is knowing what awards are out there and remembering to apply for them. However, there's a simple solution for that.

You'll have to start with doing some initial digging to find out what kind of annual award opportunities are out there for you at the local, state, and national level. Then put the info into a spreadsheet. (Yes, you can have an assistant help you with this. See chapter 5 for hiring tips.) Be sure to include what month the awards are announced, what month the applications open, and what the criteria are to make it easy for yourself moving forward. The specific dates and criteria may change a little year to year, but they generally don't change much.

"But, Kelly, I don't like talking about awards like MDRT. Nobody knows what that is anyway, and nobody cares."

I hear things like that from time to time, and although it may be true that people outside of this industry don't know the details about the associations and awards, they're smart enough to know that the fact that you won something is a good thing. If they see a list of your awards, they're not going to think, "Hmm, that's a lot of awards, but I wonder what they're even for. I wonder if they're really impressive or if they're super easy to qualify for. I should probably look into it further." Nope, they're going to see your list of awards and accolades and think, "Wow, she's a great advisor," and move on, giving you one more check in the yes column.

FREEBIE

To download our guide "Common Awards for Financial Advisors" including eligibility criteria and how to apply, visit TheReferralMagnet.com.

PRESS RELEASES

Once you win an award, the next step is to run a press release.

Press releases are a great marketing tool because they achieve many things at once: they build credibility, improve search engine rankings, and help with your social media presence. Whenever you do something newsworthy or brag-worthy, like hiring a new associate, receiving an award, or being recognized for your efforts with a local charity—anything that is a good reflection of you and sends the right message of you being successful, growing, sought after, and a good person—you can turn it into a press release.

There are two approaches with press releases, and they have different goals and outcomes. The first approach is when you go after getting local publicity. If that's your goal, the best thing to do is to find the right contacts at your local newspaper or TV station and send them your release in a format that makes it as easy as possible for them to run it. For example, I always make sure that the press release is written in the right tone and that it's carefully proofread and error-free so they can quickly publish it without any work on their part. I also include a picture just in case they want to use that as well. I'm saving them the step of having to contact me or do anything extra, and it makes a big difference in terms of how often my releases get published. I also send a thank-you note every time a local media outlet covers one of my releases. It's a small gesture, but I think it makes a difference, too. And it's the least I can do since the publicity is free.

The second approach—and the one I recommend most often to help my clients generate and convert referrals—is online press release distribution. With this approach, you develop a press release, submit it to a press release distribution service like PRweb.com, and pay them a service fee to send it out. The press release will be sent to thousands of online news outlets across the nation, and usually a few hundred of them will pick it up and run it on their websites to fill their available space.

When those outlets run your press release, each one generates a link back to your website. When you have legitimate, reputable news organizations creating links from their websites to yours, it helps with your search engine rankings. So if you want to rank higher on Google, this is a fast-track way to do so.

But the benefits don't stop there. After that, you'll get a list of every website that picked up your press release, and you can look at them and choose the most impressive one—either a newspaper in your local area or a well-known name, like the *Miami Herald* or *The Boston Globe*. Then you can create a press section on your website and start promoting them—for example, "Joe Smith was recently featured in *The Boston Globe* online. Click here to check out the article."

The average consumer has no idea how any of this happens. All they think is, "Wow, he was featured in *The Boston Globe*. That's impressive!" That credibility boost absolutely helps with the vetting process. And you will most likely have a few positive things every year that can be used as a press release. So if you get in the habit of doing this, you can build up a *very* impressive press page.

I'm still not done with the benefits, though. Once you have that link on your website, you can share it on all of your social media platforms with all of your client connections. "Check out this article about a national award we just won on *The Boston Globe* website! We're super excited, and we want to say thank you to all our wonderful clients." (And this is a great time to boost your post and make sure it gets in front of all your connections.)

When you post something like that, you'll have clients who share it because they're proud of you and of their decision to work with you, and that exposes you to new people in their social circle who might become your next clients.

ARTICLE MARKETING

Have you ever read an article that quotes a financial advisor and wondered how they got to be the expert in the article? Well, you're about to find out.

When journalists and reporters are working on stories, they often want to include the perspective of a subject matter expert in order to bring a layer of credibility to the piece. For example, they may be tasked with writing an article about how the different generations prepare for retirement, and they want to include a few quotes from an advisor who can offer some firsthand perspective.

What they will generally do is use a service like HARO (which stands for Help a Reporter Out) to recruit an expert. They'll post about what kind of story they're writing, who their demographic is, any specifics about what they need for the article, and then they'll give an assignment: "I'm doing a story for *Forbes* magazine about the different ways baby boomers, Gen Xers, and millennials prepare for retirement. If you'd like to be featured in the article, send me a paragraph about you and some firsthand examples that you've seen with your clients in all three generations."

The reporter's inquiry will be emailed out to everyone who subscribes to HARO, and if you meet the criteria, you can respond directly to the author, and if you're lucky, you'll be the one she chooses to quote.

I once asked a reporter on HARO how many responses she gets, and she said she receives about a hundred responses for each article in the first day alone. In other words, the competition is intense, but there are some tricks to help you increase your odds of being chosen.

First, you have to be fast. If yours is one of the first responses they receive, you have a *significantly* higher likelihood of being picked up because once a busy reporter receives a response that is good enough, they move on. The best approach is for you or somebody in your office to check your email or log into HARO a few times a day to see if there are any good inquiries to respond to. Then you have to be in a position where you can drop everything and quickly provide a response.

Second, you have to be good. You need to be a decent writer so that the responses you give can easily be quoted in an article. The journalist isn't looking to dig for an answer or do a lot of heavy editing.

This obviously isn't for everybody. The people I've seen have the most success with article marketing are financial advisors who have hit a level of success where they have more free time during the day. They're not working a full-time, crazy schedule so they can be Johnny-on-the-spot. It also works well for people who have an assistant, full-time marketing person, or help from a marketing agency who can do the responding for them.

It may sound like a big pain, but one thing to keep in mind is that you don't have to do it forever. These articles have a fairly long shelf life, so every time you're quoted in one and you put it on your website, it's like gold in terms of credibility building. You can do it for a little while, get a handful of impressive articles on your press page, and be done for a good long while. The people who are vetting you on your website will see the list of articles on your press page and draw the conclusion that you're a very successful advisor, and that'll be another check in the yes column for you.

PUBLISHING YOUR OWN CONTENT

Some people really enjoy writing and are very good at it. If that's the case for you, you can also build credibility by publishing your own content; it's an even better credibility booster than press releases, article marketing, or anything else. Writing your own content gives you the same benefits of increasing publicity and getting your name out there, but it also showcases thought leadership.

Huffington Post and similar online publications are always looking for new contributors. Depending on the size of your market, a local newspaper may be interested in having you write a recurring article once a month; they're always looking for good content. You can also look for blogs that are in your niche. For example, if you work with physicians, there's a very successful blog called KevinMD.com that gives advice about money, life, and business specifically for physicians. Blogs like this exist for almost every market, and you can ask the people who run them if they'd be interested in having a guest contributor.

The biggest rule of thumb if you're writing your own article is to resist the urge to use it as an opportunity to sell—not even saying, "If you want more information, go to my website." Self-promoting is not thought leadership, and this is purely an opportunity to educate. If readers are impressed with what you have to say, trust me, they'll Google and find you.

CHAPTER SUMMARY

→ Showcasing your awards and accolades the right way is *not* bragging, and people *do* care. It reminds clients that they made a wise decision, and it opens up an opportunity to share you with their inner circle.

→ Fake reviews—and real reviews from family and friends—are highly likely to hurt your digital presence and your brand. Just don't do it!

→ A feedback portal lets people know you care about your service, opens up an opportunity for new reviews, and allows you to respond to and fix situations that you may not have known about otherwise.

→ If you are allowed to use testimonials, do it. If you can't and you also can't employ case studies or client profiles, try award marketing, press releases, or article marketing.

→ Whenever you do something newsworthy or brag-worthy, you can turn it into a press release to help with your credibility and SEO.

Credibility is a key component in the referral conversion process, and there are a lot of different ways you can go about increasing yours and standing out from the crowd.

We've talked about how to impress people online, but what are some things you can do to enhance your brand when you see your clients in person? Chapter 12 will help you learn how to roll out the red carpet and create raving fans with every client experience.

CHAPTER 12

ROLL OUT THE RED CARPET

James and Heather are married forty-somethings who run a very successful financial practice in Seattle working with young, hip technology professionals.

When their practice first started growing in this market, they decided to hold an annual client dinner at an in-demand, swanky restaurant in the heart of downtown. They knew it would be expensive, but they wanted to make a statement and have a really fantastic night.

They sent professionally designed invitations to all of their clients and their spouses—several hundred people—inviting them to the hot new restaurant they rented out. They dropped tens of thousands of dollars on this one event, but they figured the opportunity to spend time with their clients would be worth it.

What they found out that night, however, is that having an event with several hundred people in the same place is like hosting a big wedding: you don't get to talk to anybody. Even making the rounds to try to speak with everyone meant that they spent only a couple of minutes at each table before being pulled in a different direction.

Sure, their clients had a nice, impressive, swanky evening on them, but it didn't do anything at all to strengthen their relationships. Their hope was that in the aftermath of the event, they'd get an influx of referrals from the attendees, but they didn't end up getting *any*—and they learned an expensive lesson the hard way.

WOW 'EM!

The experiential part of your brand, which we discussed in chapter 2, is essential for generating referrals, and it's an area that many people neglect or don't understand. Experiential branding doesn't necessarily mean fancy dinners and expensive parties that rival weddings. The most important part of the experience of your firm is the day-to-day interaction they have with you and your team—the friendly receptionist and promptly returned phone call—those things that make them like you and be satisfied with your service and that contribute to their referring people to you.

I often use Chick-fil-A as an example of experiential branding because it's the only fast food place I know of where people will actually talk about the experience in a positive way. You don't hear people say, "Man, it's so nice to go to McDonald's," or, "Wow, every time I go to Arby's, I walk out in a great mood!" Don't get me wrong, it's not that McDonald's or Arby's are bad. They meet the requirements of a fast food establishment, no more and no less. When you go to Chick-fil-A, however, the experience is above and beyond. Everything is clean, there's mouthwash in the bathrooms, the staff says "my pleasure" when they bring the food to you, and they give you those amazing mints when you're done. If you have a small child in tow and you have to wait for your food, they bring you a free cup of Cheerios to prevent a fussy meltdown. They go so far above and beyond that you walk out of there saying, "Wow, that was amazing."

RECOMMENDATION

If you want to learn more about giving your clients an above-and-beyond type of experience, I recommend *Raving Fans* by Ken Blanchard. It's a quick, easy read that gives a lot of great advice about going above and beyond.

People don't talk about fine; they talk about outstanding. That's how you want your clients to feel after every experience they have with you and your office. Every time you see them in person is an opportunity to take a step into the "wow" category—or a step away from it.

It is definitely possible to lose people based on their in-person experience. Some of the things that could push a client over the edge and lead to their leaving you include not doing what you say you're going to do, dropping balls, not returning calls and emails promptly, not being prepared in meetings, or canceling often at the last minute. Basically, anything that lets them feel like they're not getting what they need, whether that's in your core function—the financial advising side of things—or with your customer service.

You already know that, though. You're a successful advisor and keeping clients happy means being on your A game. But keeping clients happy to the point that you regularly get referrals that convert—that means being on your A-plus game.

In this chapter, we're going to look at a few ways to make your existing clients feel special so that they remain raving fans: in-person meetings, client events, and gifts.

IN-PERSON MEETINGS

The in-person meetings you have at your office with your clients are more than just an opportunity to do business with them. When you welcome clients into your space, it's a chance to strengthen your relationship and help them feel like they chose the right person as their advisor. By putting a little thought and effort into the details, your meetings can provide an experience that will make them become raving fans who are excited to refer you to everyone they know. In this section, I'm going to give you some best practices that will help you take your meetings to the next level.

ROLL OUT THE WELCOME WAGON

If you have a receptionist or other staff members, the experience of your meeting actually begins with them. Your clients should be greeted and welcomed right when they walk in the door—someone should stand up, smile, look them in the eye, and shake their hand—and they should feel like you're expecting them. Not, "Hi, how can I help you?" but, "Hi, are you Jane? Let me show you back to Joe's office." You know the old saying that everybody's favorite word is their own name? Well, I don't know if that's true, but I do know there's definitely something powerful and personal about hearing your name.

There's also something powerful about seeing it. I have a few clients who keep a chalkboard or whiteboard in their reception area where they write the names of who they're greeting that day. It's a small touch, but it makes people feel special. I also have a client who has a large screen in his reception area, and if you walk in for an appointment with him, you're going to be welcomed by name on that screen. The screen and mount cost him a few hundred bucks, and it takes him less than thirty seconds to customize the names before each meeting. Good use of time and money, if you ask me, but the bigger takeaway is that you want to be prepared for people and you want them to know it.

IF YOU'RE ON TIME, YOU'RE LATE

In addition to greeting people by name, being prepared also means being early. I had a college professor one time who started the semester by saying, "In my class, if you're early, you're on time. If you're on time, you're late. And if you're late, don't bother coming at all." I've always thought that's really good advice for important meetings, and I try to live by it myself. The reality is, there's always traffic or other meetings that run late; you just have to plan ahead and add some margin to your schedule. When you have a client coming to your office, you should be ready to get started at least fifteen minutes before the meeting. That way, if your client arrives early, you can start right then and not leave them waiting.

ALWAYS BE PREPARED

Before a client meeting, you or your staff should have already done your prep work so that when your client arrives, you're organized and ready to go. All the documents and everything you might need for the meeting should be printed (on your branded letterhead, of course!) and set out in your conference room. You should have the full client file in front of you in case you need to reference something that comes up in conversation that you weren't expecting, and you should already be logged into their digital accounts.

OFFER SNACKS AND DRINKS

Anytime somebody comes to your office, you should have a variety of snacks and drinks on hand to offer them. If it's a morning meeting, set out some pastries and have plenty of coffee and tea on hand (with a variety of creamers and sugars to suit different preferences) along with soda, water, and maybe even energy drinks. If it's a late-afternoon meeting, offer a glass of wine or a caffeine-free soda. The important thing here is the thoughtfulness of having something to offer them, not the specifics of what you offer.

PRO TIP

If you are meeting with someone you don't know very well yet, they may decline because they're not comfortable and don't want to be a nuisance, even if they really do want something. To prevent that, just grab something to eat or drink yourself, and that usually does the trick.

Whatever you offer them, be sure to make a note about what they chose so you can have it on hand again for future appointments.

One of my clients told me that her daughter got some Jelly Bellies in her Easter basket and didn't like them, so my client brought them to the office and put them in a crystal dish on her conference table. One of her clients who came in that day took a handful and said, "Oh my goodness, I'm obsessed with these!" From that point forward, every time that client comes in, she makes sure to have her crystal dish filled with Jelly Bellies just for her. It's a small gesture, but it really matters.

FREEBIE

If you really want to take things to the next level with having food and drinks on hand, download our "Client Favorite Things" template from TheReferralMagnet.com. It's a document for your new clients to fill out during the onboarding process that asks them about their favorite drinks and snacks so you can have them on hand for meetings, and it also asks for other favorites like hobbies, restaurants, and sports teams. That way, you have a go-to sheet for your meeting refreshments as well as gift ideas and conversation topics.

TAKE TIME FOR SMALL TALK

When a client arrives for a meeting, don't jump right into business unless you have no choice. Ask them up front, "Do you have a hard stop time today?" Their answer will let you know whether they're pressed for time and how quickly you need to get down to business. If they're not short on time, then don't skip the small talk. When it comes to building relationships and getting referrals, it's one of the most important parts of the meeting, so spend some time asking them about their life and how things are going. Most people love to talk about themselves and they'll welcome the opportunity to do so.

If you can help it, try not to schedule meetings back to back so that you don't end up in a situation where you have to rush things along and skip the small talk. However long you expect a meeting to last, block your calendar for double that time so you have a buffer and can deal with whatever comes up. Your client may want to have a serious or deep conversation, and you don't want to have to cut that short. If the meeting doesn't go long, then you'll have some bonus time in your schedule to check emails, return phone calls, or do some social media commenting like we talked about in chapter 9!

GIVE YOUR UNDIVIDED ATTENTION

This may seem obvious, but I'm going to say it anyway because I know so many advisors who break this rule. When you're meeting with a client, give them your absolute undivided attention the whole time. Do not step out for anyone or anything, and do not take phone calls or deal with text messages. In fact, it's best if don't have your cell phone with you at all, but if you can't part with it, at least keep it out of sight and out of mind. You don't want them taking calls and texts while you're sitting there twiddling your thumbs, and they don't want you doing it either.

The only exception to this rule is if you have some sort of family or medical issue that requires you to be on call, like if your child is sick or you're waiting on a call from a doctor. If that's the case, just explain the situation ahead of time so your client knows why you have your cell phone out and might have to step away for a call.

HAVE A MEETING AGENDA

Agendas are great for guiding the discussion topics in your meetings, and having one prepared for each meeting makes a great statement about your professionalism and service standards. Some agenda best practices for advisors are:

→ Personalize it with your client's name and the date of the meeting.
→ Outline the topics you plan to cover.
→ Include a miscellaneous section on the agenda so you can cover other topics that may come up as you meet.
→ Send it to your client ahead of time to make sure everyone is prepared.

SHOWCASE YOUR SERVICES

Along with your agenda, it's also a good idea for review meetings to have a printed document that lists all the services you offer, checking off the ones they're utilizing. This is the same tactic I mentioned in Chapter 10, and it keeps your services in front of them so they can see not only what they're already doing, but what else you offer that they're not taking advantage of.

My client Max has another way to showcase his services. Whenever a client comes to his office for a meeting, his receptionist greets them by name, walks them back to the conference room, and says, "Max will be right with you. Let me go get him." While they're sitting there before Max arrives in the room, they are a captive audience to a screen on the wall that scrolls through a slide show promoting all the services he provides. He's told me that when he walks into the room, his clients will often say, "Hey, Max! I didn't know you did..." And just like that, a conversation leading to new business and referrals begins.

SEND A FORMAL INVITE

This last tip I'm including is totally optional, but I wanted to share it anyway because it's interesting and unique.

I met an advisor one time who told me that he used to struggle with clients not responding when he called or emailed to schedule annual meetings, but then he changed *how* he was inviting them, and it made all the difference. Instead of just emailing or calling, he actually sends his clients invitations in the mail. And we're not just talking about regular invitations, by the way; we're talking about formal invitations on fancy stationery with foil-lined envelopes and RSVP cards! They are modeled after wedding invitations and they say things such as, "George and Stephanie, you are cordially invited to attend your annual review," followed by the time, date, and location information. If the date and time doesn't work, the RSVP cards allow them to write in something different that suits their schedule. He told me that almost everyone RSVPs and comes in for a meeting.

Sending formal invites to a standard meeting is certainly an above-and-beyond move that will make an impression. It made his clients feel like royalty.

Hopefully, these tips and ideas have gotten your creative juices flowing on how to roll out the red carpet and give your clients the kind of VIP treatment that turns them into raving fans. I encourage you to always be looking for ways to do things just a little bit better, to make things just a little more personal and special for your clients when they come to see you. The time and effort you spend will be well worth it!

CLIENT EVENTS

You always want your clients to have an outstanding experience when they meet with or talk to you—that's the baseline service standard. Client events, however, provide a bonus opportunity to add something special to your relationships and take them to the next level.

Remember James and Heather who threw the overly expensive night out that didn't result in a single new client? Well, they learned from that experience. Now, instead of throwing one huge event, they do multiple events throughout the year with different, more manageable groups of people—twenty to thirty instead of two hundred to three hundred. With these smaller, more intentional events, James and Heather have more time to spend with everybody, and their clients enjoy it more than the big dinner. Depending on the group they're inviting, they've done things like going to Seahawks games, hosting cooking classes with a local chef, and doing sunset sailing charters. They've become known for their unique events, and they've seen a spike in their referrals since they started doing them.

Advisors often think about client events being centered on meals or big parties, but I encourage you to think outside the box. Instead, you might try a wine tasting at a local vineyard, renting a box suite at a concert or sports event, or even chartering some hot air balloons for a sunrise flight. Smaller events also allow you to better focus on who you invite; make sure people will get along well, or choose clients who need a little extra TLC.

With client events, you don't have to do anything super elaborate or expensive. My client Melissa does simple events every month with a small handful of clients, and she encourages each of them to invite a friend to tag along. She works with a lot of women, so she does things like cooking or gardening classes, wine tastings, and even self-defense lessons. Her clients have such a great time, and Melissa gets exposure to new people she's not already working with. Through these get-togethers, she's gotten new clients and made new friends—the best of both worlds!

One of the bigger financial firms I work with hosts a Financial State of the Union event every year at their local country club. The room seats 250, and they invite their top 100 clients and encourage them to bring some friends. It's a big event, so you wouldn't think it would work to generate new business, but the reason it does is because it's not just a social event. As everyone enjoys their cocktails and appetizers, the two founding partners of the firm give a presentation about all the trending financial topics and what they expect to see in the year ahead. When they're done, they put their phone number up on the screen in case anyone has questions or wants to discuss their own situation. Do people actually call? Yes, they do. In fact, this event generates nearly 20 percent of their new business annually.

GIFTS

As an advisor, you're familiar with FINRA Rule 3220 that limits the value of the gifts you give to your clients. Your broker may have their own rules and limits on gift giving, so before you implement anything in this section, make sure you know the rules for your situation.

Because of the rules, and perhaps their own budgetary constraints, some advisors choose not to give gifts to their clients at all. But taking that stance can cause you to miss out on some great relationship-building, referral-generating opportunities.

Gifts can be an opportunity to show your clients that you're thinking about them at certain times—on the anniversary of their becoming a client or on their birthdays, as examples. A basket of fruit or cookies at Christmas is fine, but anyone can do that (and it can be costly when you think about how many clients you have). You aren't going for easy and impersonal; your gifts should be thoughtful and tailored to your clients. I have a client who sends a fresh pie to his top clients the day before Thanksgiving to say how thankful he is for them.

It's useful to have some go-to gifts that you can send for different occasions. They don't have to be expensive to be meaningful. If a client has had a family member pass away, you can use my go-to gift for such occasions—a Christmas ornament engraved with that person's name on it. It's a gift that costs $10 or $20, and it shows that you honor their loss and recognize that the holidays are a hard time for someone who is missing a loved one.

I have go-to client gifts for most occasions—weddings, babies, serious illnesses, company milestones—and you should as well. Trust me, it makes it so much easier to take action and get something in the mail when you don't have to figure out what to send. If the go-to gifts don't have to be personalized, you can even buy them ahead of time and keep some on hand.

If you serve high-net-worth clients, gift giving can sometimes be intimidating. What do you buy someone who can buy themselves whatever they want? With the advisors I work with, I've even thought that myself at times, but it's not the right way to look at it. The gifts you give don't have to be elaborate or expensive; in fact, some of the most thoughtful gifts people enjoy receiving are books. I have a client who sends out two books every year to his clients who are all high net worth. He sends one at the beginning of summer for a beach read and one at Thanksgiving with a card thanking them for being a client. The books aren't about finance or money or anything like that; they're typically inspirational, motivational books with general life advice, chosen from the bestseller lists. And, by the way, it's a good strategy to send gifts at different times of the year other than at Christmas because it cuts through the clutter.

Another client also sends books, but he sends them based on conversations he has with his clients. If someone mentions they're going through a divorce, he has a book for that. If they've lost somebody, he has a book for that, too. He did some research and created a list a long time ago of the best books for different life situations. All he has to do is check the list when something comes up and he knows what to send. Very thoughtful.

RECOMMENDATION

If you want some good go-to gift ideas and a system that makes sending them easy, check out services like Givenly and Sendoso. They are great resources that make it really easy to send gifts to your clients to help build and strengthen relationships.

As an advisor, you work with your clients through some of the biggest highs and lows in life. Since you're connected to their major life events, you have a natural opportunity to show how much you care.

ABOVE AND BEYOND

Going above and beyond doesn't have to cost a lot of time or money; it usually just requires a little more attention and focus on your clients—and it makes all the difference in the world.

This is a service business, so ask yourself, "How can I take my service to the next level?" I guarantee that using some or all of these will knock your clients' socks off and generate more referrals than ever before.

CHAPTER SUMMARY

→ People don't talk about "fine" or "good enough," so you have to be better than that. Every time you see someone, even for a client meeting, ask yourself how you can wow them.

→ If you're going to host a client event, think outside the box. Smaller, more intimate events tend to be more successful than large gatherings where you can't spend time with everyone.

→ You work with your clients through their best and worst times. Since you're connected to their major events, you have a natural opportunity to show you care. Come up with a list of go-to gifts for every occasion to make sending something as easy as possible.

CONCLUSION

As a financial advisor, you spend your days helping people—helping them make money, manage money, and leave a legacy—so they can ultimately fulfill their life's purpose, whatever that means to them. As a direct result, your clients are able to do more, make a bigger impact, and live their lives to the fullest without as much worry.

Now it's your turn.

If you've made it to this point, you've probably already realized that there is a big difference between simply *getting* referrals and being a Referral Magnet. As the latter, you get to work with the people you *want* to work with—not having to settle for working with not-so-nice people, and spending more time doing things that matter to you away from the office. You enjoy the process of helping people even more. And most importantly, you can take pride in doing what you love, knowing that your brand looks good, your clients love you and love working with you, you're making more money, and you're finally able to live *your* best life.

That's what I want for you.

In this book, you've learned everything you need to know to become a Referral Magnet. Now it's time to put it into practice.

THE REFERRAL SNOWBALL

When you implement what you've read here—even if you do only some of it, just modifying a few small things—you can build a referral-only practice where you receive and convert so many referrals that you never have to pursue any other method of getting clients. The number of people reaching out to you will skyrocket. And I hope that the process of building these new client relationships, as well as strengthening the relationships with your existing clients, is enjoyable.

I've told you before that there's no magical thing you can do to get and convert referrals. It's not about that; it's about doing everything a little bit better to elevate your business standard and do business at a higher level. The result of that is like magic.

When you make even one client a little happier, they are more likely to refer someone else to you. That new person then becomes a happy client, and then you have two people referring. Then those two people both refer another person or two, and it continues to grow exponentially. (I'll let you do the math.) You should never look at a client as a single client; you should look at every client as potentially a hundred clients—each client a snowball ready to roll bigger and bigger.

In *The Compound Effect*, Darren Hardy asks readers if they would rather have $1 million today or take a penny now and double that amount every day for a month. Most people choose the million-dollar option, but if you choose the compounding effect, on day thirty you would receive $5,368,709.12—all from one penny doubling over and over again. Every client you have has the potential to be that doubling penny!

Small adjustments net big results, so get started, open the floodgates, and drastically grow the number of referrals who are calling you, presold, already trusting you and believing in you, and ready to do business with you!

ONE BITE AT A TIME

What you've read in this book may be a big paradigm shift for you, and if so, you might feel a little overwhelmed. With so many different things to implement, it can be really hard to know where to start.

Just like anything in life, you eat an elephant one bite at a time. Take baby steps and don't let the magnitude of changing what you do prevent you from getting started. Yes, the more of the advice in this book you implement, the better your results are going to be. But even if you start with one or two pieces, you're going to have a net positive result just with that.

Change as much or as little as you want in your practice. Small bites add up to big bites, and they're all going to make a positive impact in your business. There's nothing more powerful than the exponential growth that comes when you don't have to prospect anymore, and your practice still continues to grow every year. At that point, you can officially consider yourself a Referral Magnet.

When you truly care about people, do right by them, and build relationships with them, they'll be confident sending their friends and family your way, and you'll be helping an ever-widening circle of people, the effects of which will be felt for generations to come.

What could be better than that?

ACKNOWLEDGMENTS

This book is a God thing. How it came to be is too long of a story to share here, so I will simply say that God is good, and I am eternally grateful for His presence in my life. There are also many people who made this book possible, and I could not have done it without each of you.

First and foremost, I want to thank Coby, Dane, and Aspen. You allowed me to step away from my duties as a wife and mom for countless nights and weekends to bring this book to life, and I could not have done it without your support and encouragement every step of the way. Thank you for believing in me and being enthusiastic about the book no matter how long it took me to finish it. You never lost faith in me, and I will never lose faith in you.

To my mom and dad, I wish you were here to see this dream come to fruition, but I know you're smiling down on me now. Thank you for every ounce of love and wisdom you gave me through the years and for encouraging me to dream big and believe in myself.

To the rest of my family, you have been there for me in the best and worst of times, and I would not be half the person I am today without your unconditional love and support over the years. Grant, Claudia, Mel, Mike, Amber, and Braylon—I love you with all my heart. I want to give a special thanks to Grant and Claudia for all you did to help Coby and me get on our feet when we moved to Oklahoma. Our agency and this book would not exist if it weren't for you.

To the Lawton Marketing Group team, I was able to take time away from the agency to write this book because you kept the ship sailing without me. Thank you for that and for choosing to use your God-given gifts and talents at our company. I cannot imagine working with a better group of people, and I am so grateful for our LMG family.

To my clients, I am truly honored and humbled to work with such amazing and accomplished people. Helping your business grow and thrive brings me so much joy, and I am grateful to you for trusting me with your brand.

Finally, I want to give a special thank-you to Jenn Montgomery, Jenny Shipley, and Chandler Scarbrough who each played a direct role in getting the content of this book out of my head and onto paper. Thank you for helping me bring *The Referral Magnet* to life.

ABOUT THE AUTHOR

For nearly two decades, **KELLY EDWARDS** has been helping business owners understand and utilize innovative marketing and branding strategies to increase revenue. After receiving a bachelor's degree in advertising in 2002, Kelly was hired as an Account Executive at one of the first all-digital marketing agencies in the nation. In her early career, she worked on accounts for large national brands such as Jack Daniels and Marriott Hotels, but her passion was always for helping small businesses grow and thrive.

In 2012, she and her husband, Coby, launched Lawton Marketing Group, a full-service agency specializing in marketing and branding for elite financial advisors. Since that time, the company has grown to a staff of fourteen people serving clients in all fifty states. They have received national and international recognition for their work, winning four Davey Awards, two Communicator Awards, a Marcom Award, and two Vega Awards as of the writing of this book.

Kelly enjoys speaking to advisors throughout the country about effective digital marketing and branding strategies, and she has a way of breaking through the clutter and making the complex simple. She's earned a reputation for giving advisors aha moments and helping them understand the power of their digital presence and how they can use their websites, blogs, and social media platforms to build and strengthen relationships, inspire referrals and introductions, attract targeted prospects, and impact their bottom line.

Outside of work, Kelly serves on many boards in her local community and is a strong advocate for public education and economic progress. She is happily married to her husband and business partner, Coby, and they have two children, Dane and Aspen, who keep them busy with competitive athletics and busy social lives. They are active in their church, Grace Fellowship, where Coby serves as an elder.

Made in the USA
Middletown, DE
20 July 2021